Beyond Performance

Beyond Performance

What Employees *Really* Need to Know to Climb the Success Ladder

Roland D. Nolen

NEW PERSPECTIVES

Published by NEW PERSPECTIVES
3 Danada Square East #132
Wheaton, Illinois 60187

Publisher's Cataloging-in-Publication Data
Nolen, Roland, D.
 Beyond performance : what employees really need to know to climb the success ladder /
 Roland D. Nolen. – Wheaton, Ill. : New Perspectives, c1999.

  p.   cm.

 ISBN: 0-9647697-5-1
 1. Success in business. 2. Success.
 I. Title.
HF5386 .N65 1999   99-60318
650.1/3 – dc21   CIP

03 02 01 00 ★ 5 4 3 2 1

To my wife, Terrie, for all her support and encouragement. To my daughters Mallory, Rayna, and Nicolette, who are my motivation and inspiration. To my mother, Mrs. Carnelia B. Nolen, for always believing in me. Lastly, to my father- and mother-in-law, Mr. and Mrs. Robert and Shirley Thomas for their tireless support from the very beginning. This book was truly a family project.

Contents

What Does It Take to Be Successful? 1

What's Really Happening In the Workplace? 13

Managers Reward and Promote the
People They Like! 17

The ABCs of Personal Image 23

Making Perceptions Work for You 33

Analyzing Your Image 37

Building and Managing Your Image 45

The Elements of Personal Style 53

Six Ways to Improve Your Style 71

A New Perspective for Minorities and Women 79

Looking at Yourself From a
Manager's Perspective 85

Working with Your Manager 121

Closing Comments 135

Appendices

Style Worksheets 139

Performance Evaluation Discussion Guide 147

Foreword

It is deceptively easy to find advice on "success" these days.

Wander through any bookstore and you'll find dozens, maybe hundreds, of works offering a staggering range of plans and philosophies. Of course, the challenge is to find your own definition of success. Some of us may see a narrow waist and protruding pectorals, or a full head of hair, as the epitome of achievement. Others are driven by money or possessions. A growing number of us view spiritual development as all-important.

Perhaps your personal definition of success includes a harmonious and mutually profitable relationship with the people for whom you work. If that's the case, I salute your good sense and your priorities. I also urge you to read and re-read Roland Nolen's *Beyond Performance: What Employees Really Need to Know to Climb the Success Ladder.* Within these pages you will find the methods and techniques you need to make your job a source of comfort, satisfaction, and financial enrichment.

Roland does not traffic in sophisticated psychological theories. His observations on life in the world of work do not come via some business school's graduate program. This is a man who has, quite literally, "been there and done that." Every scrap of advice Roland offers you has been put to work in his own career. He is, and always has been, his own laboratory.

As you open *Beyond Performance,* you should remind yourself to also open your mind. This book will challenge you to abandon pettiness, accept your colleagues, and allow your natural talents and energies to emerge. If, with Roland's help, you can achieve those goals you will find yourself more effective, more prosperous, and happier than you've ever been.

In short, you will have defined and achieved success.

— Jack Canfield
Co-author, *Chicken Soup for the Soul* Series

Acknowledgements

I would like to thank the many people who have helped me and contributed to the content of my seminars and now this book. To all of you, thanks for hanging in there with me.

For their feedback and support way back in the beginning, I would like to thank Marvin Bingham, Belinda Brooks, Harold Cooper, John Douglas, Michael Garner, Glenn Gladney, Winda Hampton, Karon Hudson-Garner, Karina Koptik, Toni Patterson, William Payne, Roderick Ragland, Carolyn Ragland, Gregory Ratliff, Jane Rein, Mark Rein, and Darren Williams.

For their support and contributions to this book, I would like to thank William J. Skeens, Alisa Speese, Bob Stanojev, and Stephanie Thomas.

For their feedback on the manuscript and/or just general all-around support, I would like to thank Walt Amos, Julia Bellamy, Ivan Brooks, Cynthia Glenn-Cotton, Dianna Covington, Janet Evans, Timothy Evans, Parimal Joshi, my nephew Terry Lee, Hitesh Leva, and my niece Ronda Lee Thompson.

A special thanks to Jack Canfield, Mark Victor Hansen, Michael Leven, and Dottie Walters for their encouragement and endorsement.

Lastly, I would like to thank my editor, John Clausen, for an outstanding job in making this book readable, Lowell Allen for his excellent interior design, and Kathi Dunn for the great cover.

Chapter 1:

What Does It Take to Be Successful?

It's late Wednesday afternoon at the offices of a mid-western software development company. A mid-level manager — we'll call him George — is sitting at his desk looking fondly at a photo of his son and savoring the boy's recent Little League pitching victory. "What an arm on that kid," he says softly to himself before turning back to the stack of paperwork in front of him.

He hears a tap and looks up to see his friend and fellow manager Jim Thomas peeking at him around his office door.

"Got a minute, George? I need to blow off a little steam."

"Sure, Jim." George says, leaning back in his chair. He smiles at his obviously distraught friend and waves him to a guest chair.

"You won't believe what just happened," Jim says.

"Try me."

"You know Bill Jackson? He's worked for me about a year now."

"Yeah, sure," George says. *"A couple of weeks ago you told me he's one of your sharpest people."*

"Well, I'm not so sure about that anymore. He just told me my new plan for product delivery is stupid. Stupid! Can you believe it?"

"Bill actually said 'stupid,' or do you mean he just implied your plan was stupid?"

"He used the word," Jim says, leaning back in the chair and gazing out at the view from George's corner office window. *"It took everything I had not to blow up at him."*

"Good for you. But, you know what? I bet after all was said and done, Bill had at least a couple of good, useful ideas."

"Well, I guess he did," Jim reluctantly agrees.

"It's kind of hard to hear good ideas from someone who just told you your plan is stupid, isn't it?" George asks.

"You better believe it! It was a real slap in the face."

"Actually, I don't think that kind of thing is all that uncommon. From what I've seen, Jim, some employees just don't get it. They just don't understand that how you do things can be more important than what you do."

"Exactly!" Jim says practically bouncing out of his chair. *"If Bill had approached it from a positive perspective by saying he wanted to offer some suggestions to help improve my plan, I would've had a totally different reaction. So, instead of my appreciating his input, I'm still peeved about his calling me stupid."*

"But it's not like he called you stupid. He called the plan stupid, not you," George points out.

"True, but it still feels like he called me stupid. After all, it's my plan."

"And you won't forget Bill's remark anytime soon, will you?"

"I sure won't!"

"You know, Jim, the amazing part of all this won't come until evaluation time."

"What do you mean?"

"When you and Bill talk about his performance, your opinion will be clouded by this incident. From the technical standpoint, Bill is one of your Top Performers, right?"

Jim settles back in his chair and nods as George continues, *"Bill won't understand why you don't rate him right up there with the best."*

"You're right. Being technically sharp isn't enough. I don't need his bad attitude and all this aggravation."

"Are you going to tell Bill how much he bugged you?"

"I'm not sure I want to bother. Maybe I will later, after I cool down. Right now, all I want to do is go home and take it easy!" Jim says as he stands up to leave.

"I understand, Jim, but if you don't tell him, he'll keep on doing stuff like this. At least, if you tell him, he has the opportunity to change. Then if he doesn't, it's his problem. You will have done your part."

"Yeah, you're right. I'll talk to him."

Granted, very few employees would come right out and announce that their manager's idea is stupid.

Nevertheless, many put the same idea across with their reactions, body language, and attitude. The employee may not get reprimanded for nonverbal negative reactions at the time, but managers imprint these messages in their memories with all the emotional power that frustration and wounded feelings can engender. Once imprinted, these unpleasant memories generally last for years as the most powerful influence on the manager's view of the employee.

IT'S ALL IN THE PERSPECTIVE

In the perspective lies the key to understanding.

When you look at things from another person's perspective, you discover a key that unlocks the door to understanding. Many disagreements and misunderstandings, I believe, are the direct result of people not recognizing and appreciating each other's perspective.

We've all had this experience at one time or another. You find yourself in complete conflict with another person. But then after you talk through the problems and understand the other person's perspective, you are amazed at how the whole situation had been blown out of portion.

Once you understand someone else's perspective, it's often surprising how clearly you see things in a new light and with a completely new appreciation for the situation. You also attack the problem with an entirely new attitude. The purpose of this book is to give you that new perspective on what it takes to succeed in the workplace.

THERE'S NO SIMPLE FORMULA FOR SUCCESS

Unfortunately, many people think there's a simple formula that, if followed slavishly, will guarantee success.

You may have even been told that if you worked hard, you'll be noticed, you'll be rewarded, and you'll eventually succeed. In practice, it's far more complicated.

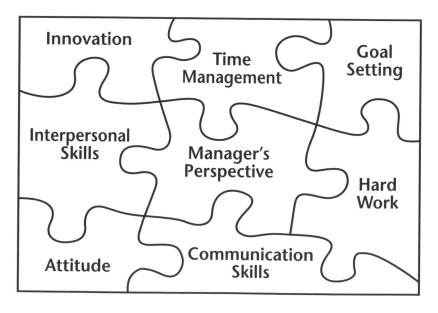

Figure 1: Example of Success Puzzle

Consider the jigsaw puzzle. In order to successfully complete one, you have to put every piece in the right place. Some pieces are larger and more important than others are, and yet they all have to be put in the right place before the puzzle is finished.

Success on the job is like that jigsaw puzzle in a couple of ways: every piece has to be in the right place, and some pieces are larger and more crucial than others.

However, there is a huge difference between those ubiquitous store-bought pastimes, and the complicated puzzle called success.

The difference is that when you buy a jigsaw puzzle in a box, you get every piece. This is not the case with the success puzzle. Many of us are never able to identify all of the pieces on our own. If we're lucky, someone may take the time to explain to us the importance of each piece of the success puzzle.

Some people are frustrated and unsuccessful — or only marginally successful — because they concentrate on only a few pieces of the puzzle.

A few deliberately ignore some of the pieces, while many others don't even realize important pieces are missing. For example, maybe you've heard that hard work, innovation, and efficiency are the keys to success.

This is true ...up to a point.

Those elements are indeed important pieces of the success puzzle. They're just not the whole puzzle.

You have probably seen people who worked hard, had excellent technical skills, and still weren't successful. Maybe it's happened to you. You worked hard but you still weren't rewarded or given the recognition you felt you deserved.

These are precisely the issues I will be addressing with this book.

In the pages that follow, you will discover several pieces of the success puzzle. However, I will be concentrating on the most misunderstood, and at the same time, the most important piece. Let's think of it as the giant centerpiece that pulls the rest of the puzzle together.

What, you may well be asking, is this huge — and utterly essential — missing piece of the puzzle? It's **your manager's perspective** on how you should do your job!

Nothing else is quite so valuable to your career as the ability to see yourself as your manager sees you.

For many of us, this is essentially a new mind-set, a new way of thinking and viewing the workplace. When you access your manager's viewpoint, you'll experience a radically different way of looking at and dealing with the people and the issues in your workplace. This is called "a paradigm shift." Your view of the workplace will no longer be limited to just your personal perspective. Instead your view will broaden to take in the entire workplace ... much the way your manager sees it.

Too many of us focus solely on our own personal perspective.

We're only concerned with meeting our own needs and fulfilling our own desires. We never stop to think about what our manager may need, or how we can help her get her job done. We are blinded by our own ambition, which, ironically, keeps us from achieving all that we could in the workplace.

When we're blinded to other points of view, we often don't grasp an important, fundamental point: ***if we help our manager, our manager will appreciate our efforts and help us.***

Managers like anyone who makes their life easier. I am a manager myself and I can tell you that nothing makes a better impression on me than an employee who understands the big picture and his or her place in it.

Once you understand your manager's perspective the fog will start to clear. You'll be able to understand and appreciate things that may have confused or frustrated you in the past and you'll definitely approach your job differently.

With this new perspective, you will have a new attitude towards your manager and your job. I guarantee it!

THREE REASONS WHY YOUR MANAGER'S PERSPECTIVE IS SO IMPORTANT

Let's look at three very potent reasons why your manager's perspective is so important to you and your success in the workplace and, indeed, in your personal life:

1. Your immediate manager has the most influence on your career success. This is especially true early in your career.

2. Studies have shown that if you're like most other employees your #1 source of job frustration and stress is your immediate supervisor/manager.

3. Regardless of how efficient you are, if your manager isn't impressed, you will not be successful. The simple fact is that if you're not doing your job the way your manager wants or expects it to be done, you will not be given the credit, reward, or recognition you deserve.

AVOID THESE SIMPLE, BUT DEADLY, MISTAKES

An astounding number of people simply don't understand the dynamics of the workplace.

I have come to this conclusion after several years of career counseling in the corporate world.

Usually, different people understand different aspects of what it takes to succeed, but few understand the importance of seeing things from their manager's perspective on a day-to-day basis. As a result, many are making simple mistakes they could easily avoid, and those mistakes are causing their good work to be overshadowed or undervalued.

Your qualities and skills are like a building; understanding your manager's perspective is your building's concrete foundation. As you can imagine, if you don't understand your manager's perspective, your building isn't built on a secure concrete foundation. It may sag here and there, or once in a while a wall may fall down. Perhaps at some point the whole thing will collapse.

Just like a building constructed without a solid foundation, if you don't understand or accept the importance of viewing workplace issues from a manager's perspective, you will always have problems.

Some you may be able to overcome, others simply won't go away.

"SELL" YOURSELF TO YOUR MANAGEMENT

During a recent radio interview, one of the hosts made this remark about my approach to success: *"Roland, you're really saying that you have to sell yourself."*

As you go through these pages you will begin to realize that by understanding your manager's perspective and adjusting your actions to accommodate that understanding, you will be building a strong foundation for your career. As the radio interviewer observed, you will be learning to sell yourself, your skills, and your potential to management.

The radio host's comment made something clear to me, something that had perplexed me for a long time.

When I first started doing my seminars, I used to wonder why some people are so much more willing than others to engage in self-inspection and are far more open to self-improvement and motivational programs.

Salespeople, it was easy to see, are definitely more prone to partake. One of the lucky things about being a salesperson is that you get immediate feedback. Either you make the sale or you lose it.

Losing a sale not only hurts emotionally, it hurts financially too. As a result salespeople feel intense pressure to examine what could possibly influence their next sale. *Did I leave something out? Did I do something I shouldn't have? Was it my attire? Was my sales pitch too hard — or too soft? Were my communication skills good enough?* Salespeople who succeed examine these things with great care before they take the easy way out and assume the buyer just didn't like the product.

People whose work does not produce immediate feedback can often be lulled into a false sense of security. They think their work will speak for itself. They mistakenly think they don't have to be as concerned about appearance, communication skills, and interpersonal skills as someone is in sales. In other words, once they're hired, they feel they don't have to sell themselves anymore. They become complacent!

Here's some food for thought.

When you're interviewing for a job, what do you do? You put on your best clothes, put together a great resume, and use your

	POOR PRODUCT	GOOD PRODUCT
POOR SALESMANSHIP	*Almost no hope of success.*	*Success depends on sheer luck.*
GOOD SALESMANSHIP	*Success is possible but not easily sustainable.*	*Chances of success are tremendously good.*

Figure 2: The Importance of Salesmanship

top communication skills to present yourself in the best possible light. In other words, you "sell yourself" to the people interviewing you.

If you sell yourself to get a job, doesn't it make sense that you'll need to continue selling yourself in order to advance in the job, or even to keep it?

William J. Skeens, Vice President at Lucent Technologies, gave the example shown in Figure 2, which further illustrates the point that salesmanship is important.

Let's examine the different combinations of Figure 2. By "Product," I mean your skills, capabilities, and how well you do your job.

Poor salesmanship and poor product: "No hope." If someone has a poor product and has no salesmanship, then the chances of achieving success are very slim.

Good salesmanship and poor product: Success is possible, but not easily sustainable. Here are the kinds of things you will hear about people in this category:
"How did he get so high up?
"I can't believe she got that promotion."

Poor salesmanship and good product: Success is possible, but questionable. It's a "hit or miss" situation. If this person does achieve success, it's often the result of mere luck, because he is dependent on someone else's pointing out his good qualities. Also, in this situation, one has to be careful in choosing a boss. Here's what you will hear about people in this category:
"Why hasn't she been promoted?"

Good salesmanship and good product: These are the true "Stars or Top Performers." Success and all of its rewards are waiting for someone with this combination of skill, personality and self promotional abilities.

THE TRUE CONFESSIONS OF A MANAGER

The best way to fully understand your manager's perspective (and its importance to you) is to break it down into its component parts. To help you accomplish this, I will focus on these three areas:

1. How your image and working style influence your manager's opinion of you and the work you do.
2. How managers think, what we expect, what we like to see, and why we may not tell you the whole truth. I like to call this part *The True Confessions of a Manager.*
3. How to make "working smart" an enjoyable, feasible part of your daily routine. You will learn to implement a program that addresses (in extremely practical ways) the day-to-day issues and problems you and your colleagues face in the workplace.

As I mentioned at the outset of this book, there are several pieces involved in solving the success puzzle. By concentrating on accessing your manager's perspective, I don't mean to imply that the other pieces of the puzzle are unimportant. Quite the contrary, I would argue that there are several additional crucially important success skills, such as time management and goal setting. I won't be covering them, however, simply because a number of excellent programs are already available on those topics. I'll recommend some of those books and tapes as we go through this book.

Learn through others' mistakes because you will not live long enough to make them all yourself.
— Author Unknown

The techniques and concepts presented in this book have been acquired the hard way ... some by the author and some by good friends who have generously shared their experiences. I hope that you will be able to use this hard-won knowledge to move your career along at the optimum pace.

WHAT MAKES PEOPLE LIKE YOU ... OR DISLIKE YOU?

Before we continue with *Beyond Performance: What Employees* Really *Need to Know to Climb the Success Ladder,* I'd like to ask you a question: Do you belong to an organization of some kind that has nothing to do with your job? It might be a civic, social, or church organization.

If you are a member of such an organization, have you worked with people on committees or teams with a common purpose? Did you find that, although you didn't really know any of them, you liked some of the people a lot and didn't like some of the others?

Why did you like those you liked, and why didn't you like the others? Past participants at my seminars have given the following reasons:

For people they liked:
• They had good ideas.
• I liked their attitude and the way they carried themselves.
• Their ideas matched my own.

For people they didn't like:
- They had bad attitudes.
- Their body language was disturbing.
- Their ideas were different. Sometimes the difference created situations where I just didn't want to be associated with them.

Think carefully about the people with whom you interact (including your managers and co-workers). Do you sometimes have negative attitudes and opinions about people, even though you don't really know them very well? If you do, take a moment or two right now to examine what inspired your prejudices.

Chapter 2:
What's Really Happening In the Workplace?

WHY ARE SOME PEOPLE SUCCESSFUL?

Why do some people get rewarded while others don't, even if they are doing the same or better work?

I'm sure many people (perhaps you are one of them) have looked at a couple of fellow workers and thought, *"I'm doing just as good a job as they are. But they seem to be getting all the credit, and they're both doing a lot better than I am. How come? Why am I not getting ahead the way they are? How come I'm not getting full credit for what I do?"*

Have you ever felt that way?

Have you ever tried to figure out why those fellow workers are getting rewarded more than you are? Could it be that:

- They have friends and relatives in high places?
- They attended the same schools as their manager?
- They belong to the right social clubs?
- They play golf with the right people?
- They belong to the same gender or ethnic group as their manager?

These factors, which I'll call "connections," have definitely helped some people succeed — no argument there. That's just the way of the world and it is highly unlikely that you will be able to single-handedly put an end to such manipulations in the workplace.

However, don't let these connections become an excuse for not making every effort to strengthen your own weaknesses. Many people succeed who don't have great connections working for them.

I know you've seen it happen. I certainly have.

It's comforting to remember that there's a flip side to the connection phenomenon: a lot of people have friends in high places, but don't go anywhere.

Here's the question we're going to pose: since many people have succeeded in spite of not having any major connections, how did they manage it? What are their secrets and how can we benefit from their experiences?

Take Responsibility and Ownership of Your Career

William J. Skeens is a Vice President of Research & Development at Lucent Technologies' wireless business group. Mr. Skeens is responsible for developing state-of-the-art wireless infrastructure products for customers around the world.

"Roland tells it like it is in the corporate world. He says to stop thinking of yourself as a victim and to start thinking of yourself as the one who has to take responsibility and ownership of your career planning and do something about it. If you take this step, more often than not, you are going to start seeing success. And because you are seeing success you are going to feel better about yourself and about your job.

"A big part of what Roland talks about is really communicating with your boss, making sure that your boss understands what your career aspirations are and what it is that you are doing in order to achieve them.

"I think Roland's philosophy says that you are the one who is in control of your career. Stop thinking that it's your management team. Stop thinking that it's some executive you barely know. You have to take control of your career. If you really embrace this philosophy, then this in itself will make a difference.

"I think Roland's concepts are really outstanding. He lets you know that not only do you have to have good performance and good skills for working with people who are significant in your career, but that you have to get these people to recognize your talents and recognize your high level of performance before you'll be able to reach your career objectives."

In other words, I want to talk about what you can do to succeed even if you are totally lacking in connections.

RECOGNIZE AND CULTIVATE TRULY IMPORTANT SKILLS

When you first started working, which skills or qualities did you think you needed to succeed? Are they the same today?

When I asked those two questions at my seminars I gained a very interesting insight. About 70% of the people who responded said the qualities or skills they had considered important success-builders had changed over time. Initially, they thought their educational level, technical ability, or knowledge was the key. After they had been working for around three to five years, they started to change their mind about what it took to be successful. They then felt the following were important:

- Interpersonal and communication skills.
- Networking with the people you know.
- Being politically astute.

WHAT'S HOLDING YOU BACK?

I've also asked seminar attendees to give me the top two factors that they felt were keeping them from advancing in their corporate environment. The most common was "nonconformity;" the second was "not being political enough." Some of the lower percentage responses were:

- Changing criteria. People felt there was always a different definition of what it took to be successful.
- Their personal career objectives just didn't match with what it took to be successful in their environment.
- They were hindered by non-supportive management.
- Management was hobbled by racism and gender bias.

Usually about 30 percent felt they were not being hindered or held back.

Let me give my personal definition of being successful: **Success is getting credit or recognition for the work you do,**

or being rewarded for it to the extent that you feel good about yourself and your job or career.

This book is dedicated to helping you take the necessary steps to achieve your own definition of success.

Chapter 3:
Managers Reward and Promote the People They Like!

To understand what's really happening in the workplace, you have to appreciate the fact that **managers reward and promote the people they like!**

Let's apply this directly to you.

You are evaluated and judged based on your manager's perception of you more than on your work. The question is, "What primarily shapes your manager's perception of you?" The answer is, "Your image and style."

Compounding this situation is the fact that what's *really* holding you back may be something that your manager does not tell you or something that you have refused to hear!

Don't misinterpret what I'm saying. Perhaps you may have felt that I was talking about superficial things, like kissing up to management or selling out. That's not the case.

In all fairness to managers, when I say you're evaluated based on your image and style, I'm not saying that managers don't value your hard work. They very much do appreciate your energy and work ethic. Think about the grid (Figure 2) we talked about earlier.

Doing good work is basic to success, but it's not the only factor involved.

Think about it this way: Everyone in the workplace works hard. Sure, there may be a few exceptions, but for the most part everyone works hard. The question then is, what separates people in the workplace?

This is where *image* and *style* enter the picture.

Managers don't intentionally or consciously mean to place so much emphasis on your image and style. But never forget that managers are human, and are subject to the same idiosyncrasies, prejudices, and inner uncertainties as everyone else. They may not even be aware that they are pigeon-holing you on the basis of anything other than the quality of your work. Bear in mind, however, that managers are quite justified in taking certain aspects of your style into consideration when evaluating your performance. We will examine these aspects in a later chapter.

MY FIRST PERFORMANCE REVIEW SESSION AS A MANAGER

To illustrate why I say your manager's perception of you is what counts, let me tell you about my first performance evaluation session as a manager.

Here's how the evaluation process worked at the time: basically, all of the managers in our department got together to discuss the performance of each employee in the department. Managers other than the employee's immediate supervisor had an opportunity to comment on each employee's performance.

Since I had just been promoted into the department a few months earlier, I wasn't all that familiar with many people in the department. As we talked about each employee, I read the employee-supplied write-up. There were many cases where, based on the write-up, I thought the person would surely be rated as a Top Performer.

To my amazement, most were considered average or "good workers" by the management team. And when I looked at the write-ups for the Top Performers, I couldn't easily tell the difference between them and the average workers. I gained some important insights from that first experience.

1. Most importantly, what's written on paper at the end of the year doesn't matter. What counts most is the collective perception that management forms about you during the year.

2. Almost as important is the fact that your good work will not get you promoted or rewarded unless it is recognizably better than that of your fellow workers. Doing your job well is not enough by itself. The people who do things above and beyond their assignments or jobs are considered to be the Top Performers. They are the ones in line for recognition and reward.

After my first departmental employee evaluation session, I started watching and listening to the way other managers described their employees and what they expected of Top Performers. Although different managers had different ways of expressing their views, over time I started to recognize common themes running through other managers' expectations. I also noticed similar themes invading my own attitudes about the employees under my supervision.

LIFE IS NOT NECESSARILY FAIR ... GET OVER IT!

Right now (this very moment) I'm going to ask you to make an important decision. In fact, it could be one of the most important decisions of your life.

I'm going to ask you to decide what's more important to you ... fairness or success. What I'm really asking here is whether or not you are able to accept that the world can sometimes be unfair, and that often you will have to make your way despite that unfairness.

Earlier, I asked if you were in organizations where you liked or disliked people you really didn't know very well. I suspect there are a few people you dislike.

Ask yourself if it is okay for you to dislike people you don't really know. Now ask yourself if your dislikes are a natural part of human interaction. When you think about it you'll realize that you're doing the same thing that your managers do. We all have a natural human tendency to make judgments about people and then put them in one of two categories: those we like and those we don't like.

Much of this has to do with their image and style. When I ask my seminar attendees to explain why they dislike someone they don't know well, they tell me, "it's the way they do things" or "I don't like their attitude."

The simple fact is that we all judge people, at least to some extent, on the basis of image and style. Generally speaking there's nothing fair about that. But what's fair in life?

DON'T WASTE YOUR TIME ON THE "FAIRNESS" DEBATE

Expecting fairness in life is a gigantic energy waster, a roadblock smack in the middle of your career path.

Let's get rid of this unhealthy notion that fairness will intercede on your behalf in the workplace. Sure, it might, but you just can't count on it and you certainly aren't well served by waiting for it. The fact is, once you're done with the fairness hang-up, you can really make serious progress.

Ask some mid-level or upper-level managers what they think it will take to get them to the next level. They will immediately tell you that the higher the position, the more promotion decisions are based on personal judgments, experiences, and prejudices. The higher you move up, the more subjective the whole process gets.

Being objective (that is, dealing with facts in a way that is undistorted by prejudices or personal feelings) only comes into play at much lower levels. A third- or fourth-level manager in a corporation will tell you *the person above you has to like you before you're going to be her or his successor.* True, there are factors like sales numbers, performance, and other things that can affect your chances of moving up to a better position. But if the person above you doesn't like you, it doesn't matter how ready you are; you're not going anywhere. Managers understand this. They know it's a very subjective process.

Only people at the much lower levels get hung up on the fairness concept.

Managers (myself included) try to make it as fair as possible. We try to make objective decisions regarding who gets recognized and promoted ... and who doesn't. The problem, however, is that any time you start evaluating people in a workplace, subjective elements come into it.

Remember, managers are only human.

Later in this book, I'm going to cover some of the reasons why a manager might like or not like you. You may be surprised and find very different reasons from what you're probably thinking right now.

A CLOSER LOOK AT WHAT'S REALLY HOLDING YOU BACK

Let's carefully examine what is really holding you back. As I mentioned earlier there are two fundamental areas to consider:

1. Perhaps you are being held back *by what your manager does not tell you.*
2. Maybe you are being held back *by what you refuse to hear.*

Let's look at each of these areas separately.

What your manager does not tell you — This may seem sinister, but your manager may not be telling you the whole truth. You may not be getting the open and honest feedback you need from your manager in order to improve. There could be a variety of reasons why your manager doesn't give you this precious feedback, and I'll be discussing those reasons later. Here again, you may be surprised to find that you may actually contribute to your manager's behavior.

What you refuse to hear — If you get the same feedback from several different managers then you'd better listen. Especially if these different managers don't know each other and you are receiving feedback from totally independent sources. Chances are you are in denial and need to admit to yourself that there must be something to the feedback. There's a good chance you have a serious problem. Maybe even more than one. I've had managers tell me how people they know are on the brink of greatness, but they refuse to "hear" (and, as a result, act on) the feedback.

Chapter 4:
The ABCs of Personal Image

Thursday morning's sun is shining brightly through the windows of George's corner office. It has been a great morning. The coffee is fresh, his tennis elbow is all but healed, and a memo of congratulations from his boss sits triumphantly in the middle of his desk.

The only dark spot on the horizon is his friend Michelle who has just arrived at George's door. Michelle, who is also an employee but not on the management level, is obviously upset.

"Hi, George, got a few minutes?"

"Yeah, sure, come on in. What's up?" George asks.

"Well, I just had a discussion with my manager, Janet. How well do you know her, George?" Michelle asks.

"I don't really know that much about her, since we're in different areas, I haven't had that much interaction with her. Why?"

"I'm just trying to figure her out," Michelle explains.

"What prompted all of this?"

"Nothing really. It's just that when I was talking to her about my performance I was really surprised when she said that I had been doing a good job."

"The last time I checked, doing a good job wasn't considered a bad thing. What's the problem?"

"The problem is I've been working incredibly hard. And I couldn't believe it when she said I was doing 'good.' I think I've been doing a great job! I've been putting in some crazy hours, and she's talking about how I'm doing good. I couldn't believe it." Michelle says, flopping down into George's guest chair.

"Calm down, my friend. Tell me exactly what she said. Maybe it's not as bad as you think."

George listens patiently as Michelle repeats the conversation between her and Janet. Michelle describes her project in detail and points out how hard she has been working trying to make sure everything goes according to plan. In fact, she tells George, she's been sacrificing time with her family to get this project done.

To make things even worse, she tells George, her manager wants even more. *"Yes,"* Janet tells her, *"you've been doing a good job, but to be a Top Performer you have to do more."*

"If I do any more," Michelle says, sinking further into George's guest chair, *"I won't even have a personal life. Is that what she wants from me?"*

"I understand how you feel, Michelle. I know you're frustrated, but I have to be careful about what I say, since I've only heard your side of the story. But even without hearing Janet's side of the story, I'm going to go ahead and stick my neck out and tell you what I think is happening here.

"Actually, what's happening to you is pretty common. I've known you for years and I've never seen you do anything but work hard. But you know what? That might be the problem. Maybe you've been working hard and not smart."

At this point Michelle starts to interrupt George, but George holds up his hand and Michelle settles back into the chair.

"I know you've heard that 'working smart' phrase a lot, but if you're like me, I didn't really understand what people meant when they said that. I just figured it was another buzzword that somebody dreamed up to sell a self-help book. I bet a lot of people looked at it the same way.

"It doesn't help that management uses that particular expression to camouflage what is really nothing more than simply overloading people with work.

"I bet you've heard one of us say something like, 'This is going to be a tough year. We'll have to be aggressive to stay competitive, so we not only have to go the extra mile, but we also have to work smart.'

"'Working smart' has been so overused and misused that most employees don't have a clue as to how to go about it! They just ignore the concept, and I really can't blame them."

Michelle sighs and rubs her eyes.

"That's great to hear a manager say," she says, *"but I still don't know what 'working smart' means to somebody like Janet."*

"I'll tell you what, Michelle, let's sit down right now and go through what it means to work smart and succeed in the workplace. We can get through some of it today, but we won't be able to finish it all today. Let's schedule a couple times to get together."

George and Michelle take out their appointment books to set up the times.

In the sessions that follow George and Michelle will explore several important areas. Among them are:

- How your *image* influences the way people think about you.
- How your *style* determines how much people like working with you.
- How understanding your manager's perspective is the key to success.

Right now I'd like you to join me in a little mind exercise.

I want you to clear your mind of any preconceived notions you may have and resist the temptation to dismiss what I'm about to say as being silly or beneath you. Believe me, it's going to sound that way at first.

As I'm working through the following concepts, I want you to picture yourself as someone else, someone who is observing you in the workplace. Also, think of the people you work with and apply these concepts to the way they work.

DRESSING FOR SUCCESS IS NOT ENOUGH

We've heard way too much over the last few years about dressing for success. It's as if all you have to do is throw on a $2,000 suit and some snappy shoes and you're guaranteed a place in corporate America.

Don't be fooled.

The way you dress is important, but it's only a small component of your image. I define your image as how you are perceived. Let me give you a dictionary definition of perceive: *"to become aware through the senses; to see; observe."*

Perception is a mental image. For this book, our working definition of the term "perception" will be, *"an image of you that others have formed based on their observations and interactions with you."*

Perceptions of you are reality for everyone ... but you!

Right or wrong, accurate or inaccurate, the way other people perceive you is reality ... for everyone but you.

If three people think you're a jerk, what's the reality for those three people? Regardless of how great a person you may really be, the reality for those folks is that you are a jerk. However they formed that opinion ... it's the reality.

At this point you may be saying to yourself, *"I don't care what other people think, as long as I know the truth, nothing else matters."*

Well, trust me on this one, there are times you should care a great deal about what other people think — especially if those other people are your management.

I think you'll agree that if your manager thought of you as Superman or Superwoman, you would be generously rewarded for your work.

FALSE PERCEPTIONS CAN SERIOUSLY DAMAGE YOUR CAREER

The real danger with workplace perceptions revolves around the fact that managers are human.

As managers, we base judgements on what we see, as well as on more subtle actions or behaviors. As a result, your manager can build a perception of you that is based on actions and situations of which you are not even aware. There is a very good chance under these circumstances that your opportunity for advancement could sustain some heavy damage. Right now you may be thinking to yourself, "I am very qualified and I do my job very well. I have a degree ... so why should I be concerned about this perception stuff?"

Well, consider for a moment the sheer power of perceptions and how your image influences the way management thinks about you. Always keep in mind the fact that perceptions can be powerful both in a positive and a negative sense. They can help you or hurt you.

Once on a television talk show, a woman was describing how she had beaten out other qualified people in her workplace based on her looks, the way she dressed, and the way she carried herself. The audience was very negative toward her. Although she was attractive, I guess they felt she wasn't that great looking.

So why was she sitting here boasting about her looks and how she beat out all those other people? What she basically said was that she had advanced past her qualified, degree-holding colleagues, based on her looks and the "way I carry myself."

The audience didn't get it.

The key to what she said was the way she "carried" herself. I sat there amazed, because I understood what she was talking about and it was obvious she knew how to maneuver in her workplace.

The Manager's Perspective

Stephanie Thomas is Assistant Director for Operation/Home Care Program, Division of Specialized Care for Children, University of Illinois at Chicago.

"Roland gives pointers for situations that make employees rethink what they are doing so that it's not an us-or-them type of mentality. He explains what management is looking for, so the employee can adapt his performance to the manager. Managers do have some pre-conceived biases when they look at employees and their subordinates. I try to just put my own value judgements in check when I get ready to assume something about somebody else, even with people on my same level.

"I think Roland's information is very down to earth and can be adapted to a lot of different situations. For a new employee or even a new manager, it would be very helpful. And, for the seasoned person, it is a very nice refresher."

The studio audience didn't give her credit for having a good grasp of how things work. She understood human dynamics; she understood that how you carry yourself makes a big difference in the workplace. By focusing on her talking about her looks, which came across as bragging, they missed the point!

Of course, someone truly skilled in the craft of communication and self-promotion might have imparted the same information without alienating the audience. Nevertheless, her point is well taken. It was her manager's perception of her that made her successful. It's really quite simple.

As I said earlier, perceptions are based on observations and interactions others have had with and of you. I'm sure the woman on the talk show had a pleasing personality, was easy to work with, and had a positive attitude. When people say "how you carry yourself," those are the kinds of attributes they're usually talking about.

Let's look at some of the unseen ways management acquires its perceptions of employees.

A manager in the defense industry told me how his company has a push for U.S. Savings Bonds each year. Few employees know this, but if you don't sign up, you get put on a list which upper-management reviews. The amount you signed up for had almost nothing to do with the way you were perceived. Someone could have signed up for five dollars a month and stayed off "the list."

In other words, employees who didn't sign up for bonds were viewed as non-team players who aren't supportive of their country. All they had to do was invest sixty dollars a year in savings bonds.

Why create this non-team player perception of yourself just to save a meager sixty dollars a year? Why get put on a list that upper-management sees and pays attention to for a savings of sixty bucks a year? It's simply not worth it. What were those employees thinking? Could it be that they didn't believe savings bonds are a good investment? Were they holding out for something that paid higher interest on their sixty bucks? Whatever the case, they were thinking in a totally different way from their management.

The following is a classic case of perception and reality not matching.

Once during a campaign for United Way, one of our upper-managers, after looking at the percentage of people who hadn't signed up, said, *"We're always being criticized for not caring about people. Why haven't these people contributed to United Way? Don't they care about people?"*

We did a survey and asked those people, *"Why didn't you sign up?"* Most of them said, *"I give to other charities."* They cared about people, they just gave to different charities. This is another case of perception and reality not matching. In this case, management perceived that the people who didn't sign up for United Way did not care about people.

Sometimes two employees can exhibit the same behavior, but management will interpret the situations differently.

Suppose Jack has a reputation for displaying a short temper in his workplace. If his manager sees him "blow up" at a fellow employee, that behavior merely confirms a previous negative perception. Now imagine that management had always perceived Jack as a levelheaded, soft-spoken diplomat and peacemaker. In that case, the behavior would be contrary to management's perception and Jack would be far more likely enjoy the benefit of the doubt.

Perhaps it's not "fair," but someone who is already perceived in a negative light will be "convicted" immediately, regardless of the circumstances.

LEARN TO PICK YOUR BATTLES WISELY

Several years ago, before I became a manager and when I wasn't considered a Top Performer, I was offered an assignment I knew was doomed to failure. I also knew my status with management at that time was such that I would be blamed for the failure, regardless of the circumstances. I also knew it would not be received well if I declined the assignment.

This was a classic no-win situation for me, but I figured I would rather take the heat for declining the assignment (because it would be sooner forgotten) than be blamed for the project's failure.

After I declined, they assigned one of their Top Performers to do it.

When the project subsequently failed under him, the blame was placed appropriately on the faulty process that was being used. I can assure you I would have had a hard time trying to convince them where the real blame should be placed. In all fairness, there is a *possibility* I could have convinced them a faulty process was responsible. But, given the situation at the time, I wasn't willing to risk it. I believed my refusal to take the assignment would soon be forgotten, but accepting the assignment and failing at it would long be remembered.

Sometimes you just have to know which battles you want to fight.

Chapter 5:
Making Perceptions Work for You

Lots of employees make small mistakes that give bad impressions and create negative perceptions.

Some innocent action or behavior may get misrepresented. In some cases, these small missteps can confirm a negative stereotype in a manager's mind. To make things even worse, many people are never told what they did wrong. You can actually create damaging perceptions without even suspecting that you're doing it.

Let me give an example.

Let's say that you're late for a couple of meetings where your boss is present, but you're *never* late for any other meetings. What's your boss's impression of you? His impression is that you are always late. A negative, albeit completely inaccurate, perception has been created in your boss's mind. You've been on time for every other meeting since you were hired, but because of an unfortunate coincidence (your being late and your boss's rare attendance at the meetings), you will have to labor under a damaging false impression.

The catch here is that you probably won't know that your boss thinks of you as habitually late because, after all, you're always on time ... except for those two times the boss was present.

Another example is the person who is always quiet and doesn't speak up to offer opinions or observations.

A manager really won't understand that you are knowledgeable if you haven't made your opinions and observations known. You're quiet, so the perception grows that you don't have anything to add to the group's efforts.

Another example: You make an inappropriate comment in some meeting and the managers there with you immediately conclude that you are not on top of the game.

Do you see how negative perceptions get started? Perceptions by their very nature are dangerous because you can't control them. In fact, in a lot of cases you really can't even address them because you don't know that they are being formed.

Ironically, it's not always the big mistakes that hurt you. Actually you can make some big errors and still get away with them. It's often just a matter of timing. You make a giant mistake and if no manager finds out about it, no harm is done. You make a minor bungle that management observes and you suffer consequences that are way out of proportion to your mistake.

The point is, you usually don't know what perceptions management has created about you, because they're keeping those perceptions or conclusions to themselves. Is management intentionally trying to keep their perceptions a secret? Not necessarily.

There could be a number of reasons why you're not told. One reason could be as simple as the time crunch under which most of us toil. As a manager, I could have every intention of telling you about something, but by the time I take care of ten tasks, go to five meetings, and stamp out a dozen other fires, I simply forget to let you know what it was that you did. Unfortunately, in an unconscious sort of way I will probably still record the negative perception in my mind

Managers also tend to have long memories. Believe me, we remember things for a long time. It's a necessary part of the job. Our interactions with many people in the workplace may be very limited. Hence, what knowledge we have about a given employee or colleague may be valuable input to a future management decision.

AVOIDING THE "WASTED YEARS"

The people who suffer from negative workplace perceptions tend to go into what I call the wasted years.

Their time and efforts aren't totally wasted, but often they do spend a lot of energy working to improve the wrong areas. This is simply because they're not being told the real story, which means that the feedback they are receiving is being filtered or altered in some way. They're not getting the whole truth, so they can't really discover why they aren't being recognized and rewarded. As a result, they're off trying to create improvements that probably won't solve their workplace image problems.

In effect, their careers are quietly being derailed.

Sometimes it takes a while for one of these unfortunate employees to realize that they are being left behind. Once that sinks in, however, despair is not far behind. Then, in the absence of accurate, constructive feedback, they will try to determine on their own what is going on.

"Why am I not getting credit for my work?" they will ask themselves. This can be a very confusing time. They realize that management doesn't appreciate their efforts, but they're doing all the things their managers said they should be doing.

Eventually, they will become frustrated and begin to search for something to blame for their plight. See if you recognize any of the following:

- **Politics** — "I'm just not political enough, that's why I'm not getting ahead. If I were more political, I could get ahead."
- **Job Assignments** — "My assignments don't give me the visibility I need. Janice gets all the high visibility assignments."
- **Friends** — "I don't have the right friends in high places. John does, and look how he's being treated. That's why I'm not getting ahead, because I don't have the friends in high places."

- **Kiss Up** — "I know why I don't get ahead. It's because I don't kiss up to management. I see Joe and Jane always kissing up to management, but I'm not going to do that, it's just not me."
- **Race or Gender** — "It's because of my race, or my gender. That's why I don't get ahead. It's just not fair."

Once an employee starts down this sort of a negative thought path he or she can easily develop a negative attitude toward his or her job, which will only serve to reinforce the poor image already existing in his or her manager's mind. Any employee who slumps into the habit of complaining and rationalizing will soon lose the ability to operate at his or her fullest potential. Performance starts to suffer and the employee begins to suspect that sinister forces beyond his or her control are at work.

For an employee going through this sort of self-doubt and turmoil, life can be full of anguish and unpleasant encounters with colleagues and managers. However, all is not lost … if the employee is willing to make the necessary changes.

Chapter 6:
Analyzing Your Image

Before you can even begin to improve your workplace image, you will have to recognize what it is right now and what areas need to be worked over. To that end, I have prepared the following image questions for you.

IMAGE QUESTION 1: ARE YOU A MORNING PERSON OR A NIGHT PERSON?

You know what I mean, a morning person is usually characterized by the expression "early to bed, early to rise." The night person follows the opposite routine ... late to bed, late to rise.

So which one are you?

If you are a night person, I have a bit of distressing news for you: *Almost all morning people think you're lazy.*

That's right, they think you're lazy. Almost without fail, if a morning person finds out you're a night person, he or she will automatically perceive you as lazy. It doesn't matter if it's your first day on the job. It doesn't matter if you're a bundle of energy who gets more done than any four morning people. You're already convicted of being lazy. I've researched this particular prejudice in my seminars and found it to be almost universally true.

To be sure, you will find the occasional morning person who takes an objective view. They understand the morning person/night person thing is just a difference in people. They probably learned this by having worked with an exceptionally energetic, accomplished night person. Positive experiences can often alter even the most closely held prejudices.

Nevertheless, the message I want you to accept is this: a large percentage of morning people consider night people lazy.

If your boss is a morning person and you are a night person, you should take steps immediately to reinforce your image as a non-lazy, productive workplace team member.

IMAGE QUESTION 2: DO YOU ARRIVE BEFORE OR AFTER YOUR BOSS? DO YOU LEAVE BEFORE OR AFTER YOUR BOSS GOES HOME?

Depending on whether you have a morning or night person for a boss, the perception created by the time you arrive and leave work could differ. Morning people are impressed by people who arrive before — or about the same time — they do.

Staying late won't impress a morning person, because they won't know how late you stayed at work. They do, however, know how late you arrived. Basically, the converse is true for a night person. They're more impressed by how late you stay.

Remember, as you go through these image questions, the techniques and solutions proposed in this book are based on the problems engendered by working for a non-objective boss. If you have a totally objective manager, your problems will be relatively few. An objective boss understands different styles.

Of course, the problem you face in the workplace is discovering if you have an objective or non-objective manager.

My advice is to play it safe!

IMAGE QUESTION 3: DO YOU LOOK LIKE YOU'RE WORKING?

Negative perceptions can be created by something as simple and harmless as casual hallway conversations ... if your manager sees you involved in them a number of times.

How does that harmless chat in the hallway look as compared to the vision of you sitting at your desk with your head down, toiling away diligently. Or how does it compare to the sight of you constantly on the rush doing something?

When you're chatting, you look like you're not working ... even if you just finished a crazed, 24-hour panic project. It creates a perception. As I said, managers base things on what they see. If I'm your manager and you don't appear to be working when I see you, what am I going to think? I'm eventually going to think that you're not a hard worker.

Here's an example from a blue-collar situation. Years ago when I was a teenager my grandfather used to tell me, "Never ever sit down on a job."

He had his own small business, and understood how things look. In a blue-collar situation, he said, even if you have absolutely nothing to do, never sit down on a job. He drilled this idea into my head. I only thought about it recently, after I began putting this book together and realized how much the concept applied.

When I was in high school, I worked at a department store. On my first day another new guy was working with me. We both worked hard and, late in the morning, we came to a point where we had absolutely nothing to do. The person supervising us said, "I'll be back in a few minutes. Just wait here." So we waited. The other guy jumped up on the table and sat down. I stood up because I remembered what my grandfather had told me. Before long, in walks the store manager, the guy over the whole store. He looks and sees this guy sitting down and he proceeds to ream him out. I mean he really went into this guy. *"Why aren't you working? What are you doing sitting down here?"* It almost got to the point of being abusive.

That same manager looked at me and didn't say a word. Not one word. The other guy quit that day; he left right after that incident.

I'd like to share another story with you. Years ago, when personal computers first came out, I wanted to copy a couple of articles to supplement my knowledge as a first-time PC owner. Back in those days, you could use the company copier. It was an acceptable perk, as long as you didn't do it during company hours.

This was during a time when my project wasn't quite as critical as some of the other projects underway in the company. Many people were putting in massive amounts of overtime. I had basically done what I needed to do for the day and was hanging around until after hours to do my copying. Sometime after six o'clock in the evening, I had copied my articles and was about to head home. On the way back to my office, I bumped into my manager. It's after hours, it's late, so what did my manager think? My presence at work said what? It said I was putting in long hours … working hard! But actually, I was only there to use the copier for my own personal purposes.

You should have seen the way he reacted! He said something like, *"It's good to see you here. You're working hard, tackling your job."*

Do you think I told him what I was really doing? I'll let you answer that one. Seriously though, that's when I first realized an important part of workplace image building: just your presence at work can create a very powerful positive perception.

That's also when the "power of perceptions" really hit me.

I then understood what probably had happened to me a few years earlier, back when I was putting in massive amounts of overtime … when I truly was working hard! The copier incident helped me to see why my management didn't appreciate all the work I had done back then. I thought about what my schedule was like, I'd leave around five-thirty or so in the afternoon; about the same time as my manager sometimes. Maybe even walking out together.

I was going to dinner. He was leaving for the day. What he didn't know was that I was coming back. How *could* he know that unless I somehow told him?

So what was his perception? The reality was that I was coming back around seven or so, staying until ten or eleven o'clock some nights. I did this for two or three nights a week; sometimes four nights a week. Sometimes, since the project was at such a critical point, I even worked on Saturday or Sunday. Of course, my boss, with whom I walked out the door, almost certainly didn't know about all that hard work and dedication.

In essence, I was making it look too easy. His perception was this: That Nolen kid can't be working too hard since he's leaving every day while there's still daylight left and plenty to get done. Even though my timecard showed the overtime, it still didn't click with him. I could never figure out why my work wasn't being appreciated until years later, after the incident with the copier.

At a more complex level, you can be way at the other end of the spectrum and still miss the target. Suppose that you are working hard and keeping your nose buried in what you're doing and giving your managers everything they need and want. That's good, but just be sure that you keep a "big picture" perspective and avoid burning out. A burned out employee is almost never an effective, top-producing employee. The trick is finding a middle ground that showcases your dedication to your job while allowing you to maintain a healthy personal equilibrium.

IMAGE QUESTION 4: DO YOU USE THE RIGHT WORDS AND GIVE THE POSITIVE SIDE OF A STORY BEFORE YOU GIVE THE NEGATIVE SIDE?

Several years ago, I worked on a technical project with three other people in a lab environment where we tested out our product. One of the people working with us was a gentleman who had worked at several different companies. This was the "go-go" '80s, when you could change jobs and keep the old salary growing. One day he said, *"I noticed around this company the key word is progress. Every company has its own set of words the successful people use and the one here seems to be progress."*

We thought about it for a minute.

We started talking through a few scenarios and examples and thinking about what he had said. We realized he was right and had a good point. Then my friend Tony said, *"Now I understand why my manager always seems to be so happy when I'm giving him bad status about this project."*

Tony explained that every time he had to make a report, he'd say something like, *"We made some progress today,"* or *"We made a little progress, but we had these problems."* Believe me, at this point in the project the amount of progress we were making was very small.

Tony said he'd noticed that every time he'd give this bad status, or at least what he viewed as bad status, his manager would say, *"Great! That sounds good."* He could never understand why his manager always seemed to be so pleased. Then we realized that his manager was focusing on the positive side of that word "progress" and didn't really absorb the negative parts.

Now, let's turn it around and imagine what would have happened if Tony would have said, *"We had problems, twelve things didn't work, but we did get three things to work."* What do you think would have occurred by the time Tony got around to saying, *"We did get three things to work?"*

Tony's boss would not have heard it.

That's right, it would have been blocked out. It always helps to give the positive side first. As human beings, we just like to hear positive things. It gives us hope. As I said earlier, sometimes what you do is not as important as how you do it. I'm not saying that clever phrasing alone is going to make you successful, but it can make a great difference.

Do it the right way. Give the positive side of the story first. Managers just love to hear good news first.

When you use this technique (or any of the others in this book) it tells your manager that you are a student of interpersonal communications. You're a person who knows how to present information. Even if he recognizes how and why you are presenting the positive stuff first, the effect is the same.

From my own perspective, I have to admit you can still impress me by using these techniques. I know that when I walk in and see someone from my group already working, I'm impressed. I recognize what's happening, but I'm still impressed. If that same person is still working when I leave, I'm impressed again.

My point is this: Even if you have an objective boss, the tips I've given you can still help your upward progress in the company. Think about it. If you were the boss, who would you prefer to recognize and promote?

IMAGE QUESTION 5: DO YOU DRESS TO FIT THE NORM?

I've read books that advise workers to dress at the level to which you wish to be promoted. I don't think this is necessarily good, universal advice for promotion-seeking employees. If you're working on the docks and you'd like to work in the front office, does that mean you should abandon your jeans and work gloves and tote boxes in a suit and tie? Of course it doesn't.

Say, for example, that you're working in a software research and development department where everybody wears khakis and polo shirts. You want to eventually end up in the company's sales department, where the sales people wear $2,000 suits. Obviously, dressing like that would draw some unwanted attention to you in your own department.

Personally, I feel that you should avoid overdressing or underdressing. Let your work and your attitude lift you toward your future promotions

Dress in an appropriate fashion for your workplace and level in the company.

IMAGE QUESTION 6: DO YOU INFORM YOUR MANAGER OF POTENTIAL CONFLICTS OR PROBLEMS BEFORE THEY HAPPEN? DO YOU TAKE MEASURES TO ENSURE THAT YOUR MANAGER IS INFORMED?

What do you do if you're having car trouble and you know you'll be late for an important meeting? Do you call to let your boss know that you're going to be late or do you simply offer up your excuse when you get to work?

I'm the kind of manager who takes customer meetings very seriously.

Someone who worked for me showed up late for two customer meetings. I believe in giving immediate feedback, so after the second incident I called him in to find out why he was late. Before he gave me the facts, though, I wanted him to realize the perceptions his lateness had created. I told him that because he had been late for those customer meetings I had concluded that he was sloppy and undependable.

After he told me the facts, however, I completely changed my mind. His child-care situation had made his lateness completely unavoidable.

Nevertheless, even though he had a valid reason for being late, I told him that he hadn't handled the situation correctly. *"You knew you had a potential conflict that could interfere with your ability to get to the meeting on time, so why didn't you tell me so beforehand?"*

Taking preventive measures in a timely fashion creates the perception that you're responsible and professional.

Chapter 7:
Building and Managing Your Image

By asking yourself the preceding chapter's image questions, you should have been able to determine ... at least in general terms ... what kind of image you have right now.

The next step is learning how to "build and manage" your image.

The purpose of this whole "image" discussion is to raise your level of awareness regarding the subtle actions and behaviors that can influence your manager's impression of you. *Please note that I don't endorse or encourage using image as a technique or trick to overstate your work.*

With that caution in mind, here are four basic points to remember as you are building and managing your image.

1. Let me re-emphasize the point that I just made. *Never* use image as a technique or trick to overstate the value of your work. It won't work for long, and when it backfires you'll be marked as a trickster who can't be trusted.
2. No matter how skilled you become at image building, you still have to do the work! You really cannot foster a great workplace image in the absence of a solid base of good work.
3. If you have a reasonably objective manager, the task of managing your image may become somewhat less critical. Keep in mind, however, that even the most objective manager may sometimes slip into human frailty. Never take managerial objectivity for granted ... play it safe at all times! I've heard people say, *"My manager knows me, I don't have to worry about this image stuff."* Don't fall into

this trap. You can never be absolutely sure that your manager really knows and understands you.

4. Always be mindful of how your actions and behavior look to management, as well as to other people, even your peers and those working under you. A positive workplace image will make your life easier no matter where you apply it. And besides, you never know where your next manager will come from.

UNDERSTANDING HUMAN RELATIONS: HOW YOU TREAT PEOPLE REALLY DOES MATTER

> *You can accomplish by kindness*
> *what you cannot do by force.*
> —Publilius Syrus

Simply stated, your success in the workplace depends almost entirely on how you treat people.

When you interact with people, treat them in such a way that makes them feel good about themselves and about working with you. You must avoid diminishing their dignity or self-worth. The key to success in this matter is your ability to understand other people's perspectives and to control your own ego.

This is not necessarily an easy task. In fact, it is probably the basis or at least a major component of all good mental health. It's the concept behind the Golden Rule. And yet, only a small percentage of us live by it. If you've ever spoken with someone just entering the work force, you've probably heard that person say something like, *"The first thing I had to learn was that work is about working with other people."*

BEING RIGHT IS NOT ALWAYS ENOUGH

Before we go any further, I'd like to invite you to read one of the best books ever written on the topic of getting along with our fellow humans: *How to Win Friends and Influence People,* by the late, great Dale Carnegie

Reading it switched the light on for me. It was a major turning point in my life. I went from being a techie who lacked interpersonal skills and didn't know how to work with people to being someone who understood that it's all about working with people.

Before, I was one of the people who took the "right stance" referred to by Mr. Carnegie. As long as I was right, nothing else counted. Other people's feelings didn't matter. If I engaged in a technical discussion or argument with you, I'd do my best to demolish your arguments and prove I was right. Then after I chopped you to pieces, I thought you should be grateful. After all, I was right! You should appreciate my putting you on the right course.

But what really happens after I chop you to pieces? You become my enemy ... or, at the very least, our friendship is put in jeopardy.

While reading Mr. Carnegie's book, I had a weird experience, a powerful flashback to my college days. It was as clear as if it had happened a couple of days before.

I remember being in a fraternity meeting and talking about one of my fraternity brothers, who was our fraternity's basketball team coach. I remember making a statement to this effect, *"Yeah, he's a good fraternity brother, but he can't coach worth a damn."*

As you can see, the word I used was not very complimentary. Since I was right — because he wasn't a good basketball coach — I actually thought he'd appreciate my honesty. Of course, he didn't and, looking back on the incident, I can see perfectly why he resented my observation. But back then I didn't understand why he and I weren't friends afterwards. I couldn't understand his reaction. I could dish it out and take it too. So I thought other people could too.

In a way, I was using the Golden Rule: Do unto others as you would have them do unto you. I preferred that people be as brutally honest as possible with me ... as long as they were right.

What I should have been doing was using author Tony Alessandra's Platinum Rule: *Do unto others as they would want to be done unto.*

YOU DON'T HAVE TO BE CRUEL TO BE STRONG

In all business matters, treat others as they would want to be treated. If you want to be effective, you have to be mindful of other people's feelings when you're interacting with them. Being right simply will not make up for embarrassing or belittling them.

Unfortunately, this is an area where many managers also make mistakes. Think back to my department store job and the royal chewing out my fellow new-hire received for simply sitting down while we were waiting for further instructions. He felt so bad about the interaction that he quit that day. Who knows, if he had been handled with more understanding he could have turned out to be a wonderful employee. He could have been a major asset to the store. But we'll never know, because one frustrated, insensitive boss let his temper and his ego get the best of him.

Hard-case bosses, like that store manager, often believe that they can treat employees any way they want. They may even think that they are justified in being "tough." However, as Franklin Delano Roosevelt once remarked, you don't have to be cruel to be strong. He, of course, was referring to an entire nation and a world war, but the sentiment is true at every level of human interaction.

Remember this: Employees may tolerate their boss's bad behavior — depending on the level of abuse they have to take — but I can guarantee that any short-term benefit from this behavior will be nothing compared to the long-term damage.

As an interesting aside, over the years I have purchased and handed out many copies of Mr. Carnegie's book. Of all the friends and fellow workers who have read *How to Win Friends and Influence People,* only one person had a negative attitude toward the book.

He was also the only one among all of those people who later had performance problems to the point where he had to be put on probation and was quite likely to lose his job. Was he doing his work? Yes. He had been put on probation because of his poor interpersonal and teamworking skills.

Remember what I said earlier? *Sometimes the thing that holds you back is the thing you refuse to hear.*

DON'T LET THE THINGS YOU SAY DIMINISH YOUR WORK

People will always remember the way you treat them.

That goes for your peers, the people who work for you, and your own manager. Rub people the wrong way in a meeting or some other interaction with them and that's precisely how they will remember you. If you're always complaining, management will remember how negative you are, as opposed to how well you do your job.

A couple of decades ago, a friend of mine worked for a man-ufactured-housing company in Arizona. He told me about a co-worker who, although he was a kind man and a good friend, had developed the habit of complaining. In fact, he took it a level or two above mere complaining. About once a month, this poor man used to get so bitterly incensed over some real or imagined insult that he would quit his job. The manager would routinely accept his resignation and then hire him back a few weeks later.

At first blush, it would appear that the complaining worker wasn't being hurt by his odd behavior. After all, he did get his job back whenever he wanted it, and, according to my friend, his work was considered first rate by the rest of the employees.

But imagine for a moment how well he could have done if he had cleaned up his image. Obviously, management respected his abilities. Why else would they have kept hiring him back? But what sort of promotions had he denied himself by such self-indulgent shenanigans?

Management may also take comments you make and draw from them certain conclusions about you.

For example, you could make an innocent comment or joke about something, only to find out later that a manager took it out of context or blew it out of proportion.

Never forget the fact that managers are human. Like other humans we sometimes jump to conclusions based on informa-tion that may have been inaccurate or taken out of context. To make it even harder on employees who make visible mistakes, we are almost forced by time and information constraints to use that often tainted information to arrive at our decisions regarding advancement and promotions.

This flawed, human system can make life miserable for employees, but it can also affect people outside the immediate company.

A manager in the healthcare industry once told me about a consultant who fell victim to a negative image. The consultant, although she had worked with the manager's firm for years, wasn't highly regarded by the company's top management. It turns out that their unfavorable impression was based on a negative statement the consultant had made nearly a decade ago.

Since then the consultant had been doing top-notch work, but her efforts had been virtually ignored. In other words, that one negative statement overshadowed that consultant's excellent work.

SILENCE IS NOT GOLDEN

Silence, we are told, is golden.

That adage may be appropriate in many situations, but not to the workplace environment. If you're not saying anything, people will assume it's because you don't know anything. It would be nice if your colleagues would interpret silence as evidence that you already understand the topic under discussion and, therefore, do not need to ask questions or raise concerns. Unfortunately, that's not the case.

The perception is that you don't understand or, worse yet, that perhaps you don't even care. I'm sure you'll agree that's not the image we're trying to build for you here.

When I worked at IBM, I heard about a project one of our team members was working on. My fellow workers were always talking about how great and complicated the project was. When I was finally able to attend a presentation on this much-talked-about project I found it to be painfully boring. In fact, I nearly fell asleep. The project was big, but it wasn't complicated. I was actually surprised at how simple it was.

One of my team members turned to me during the presentation and asked if I understood what the project was about. I said, "Sure," and started describing to him what the project leader was doing. He looked at me in amazement because I understood so well what the project was about.

My manager overhead the discussion between the two of us and was also greatly surprised at how much I understood. At first I couldn't understand why these people were so amazed.

Then I realized what my silence was communicating. I had come across as if I didn't understand what was being presented simply because I hadn't said anything during the whole meeting. I hadn't commented on anything or given any indication that I understood what was happening. In other words, my silence was not golden.

You have to speak up.

DON'T STAND IN FRONT OF SPEEDING TRAINS

"Speaking up," is almost always a good idea. However, there are times when you will be well served by keeping your thoughts to yourself. This is largely a matter of survival ... of not antagonizing your manager unnecessarily. In other words, *"Don't stand in front of speeding trains."*

Here's what I mean. If the management of your company is planning an action that you feel would be inappropriate, unwise or even disastrous, you have an obligation to express your concerns.

However, you may end up expressing your concerns and making your case without bringing management around to your point of view. If that's the situation, leave it alone. Don't keep arguing and pushing the issue. The last thing you want to do is become negative. Begin complaining bitterly and you're standing in front of a speeding train. Believe me, you *will* get run over.

It's much better to make your point politely and forcefully and then stand back to watch your predictions come true.

Never, ever say, *"I told you so"* to your boss. Always keep in mind that there may be more global business reasons for management's action. You may not be privy to the whole picture at your level.

Chapter 8:
The Elements of Personal Style

George is walking back to his office after a particularly intense managers' meeting when he hears someone trotting up behind him. He looks over his shoulder and sees his friend Jim waving him down.

"Got a few minutes, George?"

"Yeah, I'm pretty burned out after that meeting. I could use a little breather before I go home," George replies.

The two friends take a left at the end of the hallway and head for the staff break room. George pours two cups of black coffee and looks disdainfully at a pink box half full of hardening donuts. He points to the box and raises his eyebrows at Jim.

Jim takes the offered coffee but wrinkles his face at the thought of the pastries.

"In the meeting," Jim says after he takes a tentative sip from the coffee mug, *"when we were talking about our rising Top Performers, did you notice that everyone was raving over Ronda Nelson, but Pat Johnson hardly got mentioned?'*

"I guess I noticed that all right," George says as he slides into a lime-green plastic-mold chair and puts his coffee on the table in front of him. *"Why do you ask?"*

"It's just that I think both of them are very good and do an excellent job on any assignment you give them. Why is it we seem to have a much higher opinion of Ronda?"

"Why do you think we do?" George asks.

"Hey, don't get me wrong," Jim says quickly. *"I like Ronda more, too, and I probably would promote her before I would Pat. It's just that while we were talking it occurred to me how good they both are. Then I got to thinking how Pat wasn't thought of nearly as highly as Ronda is. What is it about Ronda that we like so much?"*

"I call it her style." George explains.

"Her style? What do you mean?"

"Her style is the way she carries herself. Partly, it's how she interacts with others, her interpersonal and communication skills, and the way she does her job."

"You mean her personality?" Jim asks.

"Oh, her style includes much more than her personality, although you do need a reasonably good personality to have a good style. I've seen a lot of employees who have great personalities, but the rest of their style just doesn't cut it," George points out. *"Think about how Rhonda communicates her ideas in meetings and in one-on-one situations ... haven't you noticed how responsive she is?"*

"Yeah, I have, and I think I see what you mean now. I've noticed in meetings how she never gets upset and is always willing to listen to others. I really like the way she carries herself in meetings. And I know my team is always commenting on how helpful she is whenever anyone needs help. Great team player."

"Now think about Pat. What's her style like?" George asks.

"Well, she's a really hard worker ... but she tends to be a loner. I've also noticed that she is very quiet in meetings and sometimes you almost have to force her to give an opinion."

Jim gets up to pour another cup of coffee. *"You know,"* he says looking back at George. *"I am really starting to see the difference between the two of them and why we like Ronda so much. When you think about it, style is what really separates people in the workplace."*

"That's right!" George agrees. *"Style is the mysterious thing that causes management to like or not like an employee.*

"For example, whenever you hear a manager say something like, 'Joe is really good, but I just can't recommend him for the promotion. There's something about him, but I can't put my finger on it.' I'll tell you right now that the problem is Joe's style. I can guarantee it!"

By now George is warming to his favorite topic.

"I think style is the most important component of anyone's image in the workplace. I define it as your behavior while you're at work. Your style consists of basically two components," he says, counting off his points on the fingers of his left hand.

"One, your management's perception of how you communicate and interact with your peers, how you communicate and interact with your management, and the way you communicate your thoughts and ideas in one-on-one and group situations.

"Two, it's the way you do your job. In other words, the approach you take on assignments and tasks.

"I can give you three great reasons why you should be concerned about your style," George continues, counting on his outstretched fingers.

"One, style is the mysterious thing that causes management to like or not like you! Two, style determines how much influence you will have in your workplace, because the better your style, the more willing people are to work with you. And, three, style is the area where people seem to have the most difficulty making changes or improvements."

"You're right," Jim agrees, impressed with George's passion on the topic, as well as with his manicure. *"People don't decide to change their style quickly or easily,"* Jim says.

"But the decision becomes easy when you realize how important having a great style is to your earning capacity."

George stood up and rinsed his coffee cup before glancing at his watch. *"I guess the lecture is over. Thanks for letting me bend your ear. See you tomorrow, Jim."*

LEARN TO IDENTIFY AND FIX YOUR OWN STYLE PROBLEMS

Let's take a quick look at some of the typical style problems people tend to have. You may recognize yourself or some of your colleagues in any or all of the following communications and interaction style problems.

Your style problem could be that:

- You're too quiet.
- You talk too much.
- You don't work well with peers.
- You are a complainer.
- You don't listen or accept feedback.
- You are too emotional and tend to over-react.

From the way-you-do-your-job perspective, you could be someone who:

- Refuses to accept the political aspects of your job.
- Isn't doing the job the way your boss wants it done.
- Has poor communication skills.
- Provides status information that is either too detailed or not detailed enough.
- Has poor presentation skills.
- Doesn't do a good job on administrative tasks.
- Keeps an office so neat that it never looks like work gets done there, or one so sloppy it looks like no one could accomplish anything there.
- Is frequently late for appointments or meetings.

STYLE EXAMPLES

George hurries through the doors of his favorite cafe and spots Jim sitting at their regular table.

The glass of iced tea in front of Jim is about half full, so George knows that he's a few minutes late. He tries to apologize, but Jim is already talking to him as he sits down.

"I've been thinking about this style stuff you and I were talking about the other day," Jim says. *"It's really starting to make sense for me. I think it might be one of the most important concepts I've ever locked onto ... especially as it applies to promotions and recognition."*

Jim pauses as the waiter, whose says his name is Indigo, explains the specials. George selects a chef's salad, while Jim orders the goat jerky and rice special of the day.

"This style concept is really helping me understand some of the opinions I have about people," Jim continues after the waiter leaves. *"I've always known that I felt a certain way or had an opinion, but many times I wasn't sure why. So, the last couple of days, I've been looking around trying to determine what type*

*of style different people have and how it plays into my opinion of
them."*

"Who have you thought about?" George asks, putting down
his fork.

*"Well, first I started with the people I liked and tried to figure
out why. Take Mark Woodson, for example. You know him, right?
Now there's a young guy who's going places.*

*"He has a really good personality and people like working
with him. And to be so young ... I'm just amazed at how well he
carries himself in meetings and discussions. He never gets upset
and he's always contributing to the discussion, and he encourages
others to speak up. One time I was in a meeting with him where
he could have easily been negative toward some of the team and
he would have been justified in doing so, but instead he tried to
encourage them.*

*"He also does some other things that probably help make him
so likable. For one thing, I notice he goes to lunch with everyone ... none of this only going with certain people."*

"Yeah, I know what you mean." George says, *"Let me tell you
who I think has a great style. I wish I were as smooth as she is.
When I grow up, I want to be just like her."*

Jim grins at his friend. *"That wouldn't be our dear friend and
colleague, Brenda Robinson, would it?"*

"Yes, it would." George admits.

George, Jim and Brenda all work as managers in the same
department and for the same boss, Bob Young.

"Brenda's always punctual," George says. *"She takes meticulous notes, and she's always volunteering to help Bob with some
administrative item. Ever notice how, right before she goes home,
Brenda spends a few minutes getting organized for the next day?
She checks her calendar and tidies up her desk before she leaves;
there's never anything out of place on her desk.*

*"And the killer is that she also has a nice personality. You
mentioned how Mark goes to lunch with everyone, I noticed that
she does the same thing. But it's more than her just being nice, it's
also the way she does her job. Do you remember the e-mail Bob
sent all of us the other day asking for opinions on that new software development tool?"*

"Sure do," Jim says.

"Well, I responded by spouting off about how we have to be careful about jumping on every bandwagon that comes along. I blurted out how we need to take our time and investigate whether it makes sense for us to use the tool. Sound reasonable?" George asks.

"Yeah, that sounds pretty good. That's the way I felt about that tool too."

"Did you see Brenda's reply?" George asks his friend. *"She basically said she didn't have any experience or knowledge about the tool, but she would be willing to head up a team to investigate its usefulness to our organization. Now, let me ask you, if you were Bob, which response would you like better?"*

"Hers, of course. I see your point. She's good, all right ... very good!" Jim says as he pours hot sauce on his roasted goat.

"And then you have all these people with their poor styles, and they're grumping and growling around, questioning why they aren't recognized as Top Performers." Jim continues. *"Take Joe Townsend, for example. He really irritates me when I go into his office. He's got this bad habit of sitting at his terminal and talking to you while he works. I guess he thinks he's being efficient, but to anyone else it just seems like he's ignoring you. He doesn't understand how much people hate that."*

"I see the same thing happening outside of our company," George says. *"The other day in one of those fast food restaurants over on Speedway the guy taking my order carried on a conversation with another employee the whole time — as if I wasn't there."*

"Did he goof up your order?" Jim asks.

"No, so technically he did his job. But as a customer I didn't feel like I got the attention I deserved."

Jim quickly takes a large gulp from his water glass. *"Man, that hot sauce is brutal,"* he says as his face turns red. It's a moment before he can continue. *"I've been thinking about this style stuff a lot lately. In fact, I've come up with some names for what I consider to be the worst styles. Want to hear them?"*

"Sure."

*"**Number 1 is Ms. Doom and Gloom.** She's always negative. No matter what you or your team is trying to do, she always looks at the negative side and never thinks anything new will work. She*

always has a dozen reasons why something won't fly. Her attitude works like a wet blanket on any new ideas or projects.

*"**Number 2 is Mr. Nit-Picky.** He makes a mountain out of every mole hill. He is usually a very smart man, but he dwells on minor points and derails meetings with his constant bickering."*

George laughs out loud. *"You're exactly right! I once worked with a Mr. Nit-Picky on a design team. He was a terrible drain on the team's morale, and he always turned what should have been a meeting of reasonable length into a marathon meeting. One time his nit-pickiness kept the team from covering more than three or four pages of a design document in two whole hours. Normally the team would have reviewed the entire 40 pages in those two hours."*

George signals to the waiter for the check as Jim continues.

*"**Number 3 is Ms. Perfection, the prima donna.** Although she's not as bad as Mr. Nit-Picky, Ms. Perfection can also slow down teams with the attitude that everything has to be exactly right and done her way; otherwise it just isn't good enough. Usually these types are a little too impressed with themselves and are convinced they have all the right answers.*

*"**Number 4 is Mr. Complainer:** He's similar to Ms. Doom and Gloom, but he's worse. He's more than just mildly negative, he complains all the time about everything. Management, according to him, has never done anything right, with the possible exception of hiring him. He not only drains his manager, but he also weakens team morale by complaining about things other team members may feel positive about. Basically, he's a manager's worst nightmare!"*

"Well, you've covered the worst types," George says, grabbing his change as he stands up to leave. *"Amazing to think how many of them are out there. Probably every office has a few."*

CHANGING YOUR STYLE CAN BE DIFFICULT

Earlier, I said that style is the area where people seem to have the greatest difficulty in making changes or improvements. Here are three reasons why this is so:

• They confuse changing their style with "selling out."

- They take things too personally.
- They're too emotionally attached to the way they do things.

WHEN YOU DO THE RIGHT THING, THE RIGHT THINGS HAPPEN

When I refer to "the right thing," I'm thinking of the political and administrative tasks that people have to perform to maintain their success in the workplace.

People often mistakenly view these necessary political tasks as "kissing up" to management. They feel that their values will be compromised. Please understand right here and now that practicing politics in the workplace does not have to mean compromising your values or becoming the office sycophant.

Here's the reality: If you put two or more human beings together, you're going to have politics. Think about any group with whom you are involved, either at work or at home or anywhere else. Any time you're working with other people politics is a factor. Whether the effect of the politics is good or bad depends on the people who are involved in the group. You can make it good or you can make it bad.

Let's take a closer look at why some people refuse to be involved in good politics: There are two main reasons:

1. **They see people they don't like doing "political" things:** The workplace is full of rivalries, jealousies, and small feuds. If an employee sees an employee he doesn't like doing political things he may lump that political behavior in with the objectionable behavior that prompted him to dislike the other employee in the first place. He comes away thinking that anyone who makes political moves, no matter how effective those moves may be, is someone unworthy of trust and certainly no one to imitate. The problem is that some of those objectionable people will sometimes be doing the right political things. As the old saying goes, "Even a broken clock is right twice a day." Don't automatically disregard good political moves sim-

ply because they are being performed by people you don't like. You can learn from anyone … even your enemies!

2. **They confuse doing political things with selling out!** Practicing good politics is not selling out. Don't confuse changing your style with changing you. By all means, hang on to your moral values and guard your ethics carefully. But don't resist change just to be resisting change. The changes you may need to make, those I know of personally and those echoed in past seminars, are changes in your style only. After a recent seminar, I was approached by a young man who told me, *"I've known people who started out 'playing the game' and now they're sell-outs!"* My response was, *"If they really did sell out, playing the game initially didn't have anything to do with it. They already had a propensity to sell out, and were just looking for somewhere to do it. They would have sold-out, no matter where they were."*

ARE YOU IN OR ARE YOU OUT?

Politics are a fact of life. Once you admit that to yourself, you only have to decide whether or not you want to employ politics to further your own interests.

If you decide that your moral compass won't allow you to be involved in workplace politics, then let us hope that you are also ethically and morally equipped to accept the consequences cheerfully. You may miss opportunities, plum assignments, recognition, compensation, and promotions. It is not fair to complain about your missed opportunities if you haven't taken the logical, politically wise steps to assure your success.

In other words, find the level of office politics you find acceptable and work diligently to recognize and make the right moves.

NOTE: Few things irritate managers quite as profoundly as an employee who refuses to perform any of the political aspects of the job … but still complains about his or her lack of success.

DON'T LET YOUR EGO GET IN YOUR WAY

Style is nothing more than conforming to a behavior code. It's the way you interact with people and the way you carry yourself.

Put your ego aside and understand that you are only being asked to consider your behavior as it applies to your personal work style. Most people get their egos way too involved when management asks them to change something about their style.

For example, management may just ask them to change the way they interact with people in a meeting and they respond along these lines: *"Well, that's me. It's the way I am, the way I operate. It's my personality, the way I communicate."*

This is a very negative response.

I like to ask people this question: *"Does making a change in the way you communicate or the way you present information or the way you interact with others really change you?"*

The answer is always, "No." A simple style change has nothing to do with changing you or changing your basic moral values. It just changes the way you operate, the style you have at work. Successful style changing means giving yourself a new and more potent way of presenting your thoughts and your contributions. As a result, the people who can help you make the most of your opportunities will appreciate you.

As I was beginning to write this book, a good friend made this observation: *"The new thing seems to be style. Years ago whenever I was getting performance evaluation feedback, people told me I needed to work on my technical stuff. Now all of a sudden, I'm hearing about my style. They tell me my style isn't right and I need to work on improving it."*

This is not new. Style problems have always been there. When you first start working, typically you tend to concentrate on the technical aspects of your job. You're new. There is a big difference between the theory and concepts learned in school and the practical applications in the real world.

You could also be entering a field in which you have no training or experience, so everything is on-the-job training. Either way, you do indeed have to concentrate on the technical aspects of your job.

Keep in mind that you're just entering the work world. It's a good bet that you're bit naive, as well as somewhat over-eager. Understandably, you're trying to make a good impression. *"Work hard,"* you think, *"all I have to do is work hard."*

Initially style may not necessarily come up. If you're lucky and you naturally have a pretty decent style, it may not come up at all.

That doesn't mean, however, that you should simply ignore the issue. Just because you're not hearing about your style doesn't mean that it couldn't use some improving. A few years down the road your technical skills — as well as those of your colleagues — will have become extremely well-honed. At that point, you will be roughly equal in terms of techniques and skills. Improving your personal style may be the vital step you need to take in order to stand out from the crowd and further your career.

If you're lucky, someone will observe your style shortcomings and coach you on how to improve. Unfortunately, many people never receive this sort of coaching. If someone approaches you about your style, be grateful. They are trying to hand you the keys to success.

FIND OUT WHAT INSPIRED YOUR STYLE

What determines a person's style?

Not wanting to deal with politics may stem from the way you were raised. The concepts and ideals drilled into you as you were growing up can strongly affect the way you live your life.

Undoubtedly, your cultural background and upbringing are huge influences on the development of your working style. For example, many first- or second-generation American citizens experience style difficulties in the work place because their cultural background conflicts with American culture. Other factors that can influence your style include race, gender, and religion.

In an almost subliminal way, the media has also had a great influence on your personal work style. Think of the movie characters you found exciting and memorable. Consider the writers or musicians or comedians or other entertainers who have made an impression on you over the years. Take the movie *Animal House,* for example. I've overheard dozens of guys telling friends (usually female) that the fraternity house in that movie was "exactly like my fraternity." Of course, the guys claiming spiritual kinship with John Belushi and his co-stars probably never committed even a tenth of the small crimes and over-the-top pranks depicted in that very successful movie. The point is, the media (in this case a movie) can actually re-shape how we think of ourselves and our place within society

Here's another example. I'm sure many men in the corporate environment are drawn to the myth of the heroic cowboy drifter. These fictional gunslingers would come into town, shoot up the place, wipe out the bad guys, and then ride off into the sunset. Each of these characters was a hero who did his job and put up with no nonsense from anyone. He made his moves according to his own code of ethics and then went on his way with everybody's hearty thanks ringing in his ears.

There are people in every company who want to be the loner; whose attitude is, *"Don't bother me as long as I'm doing a great job."*

Many men believe in this style and a lot of them bring the loner attitude to work. Almost immediately there's a conflict, because everybody in the workplace has to interact with other people. Being the loner simply doesn't work. Granted, it may appear to work occasionally, but don't bet on it as a career choice.

Now let's talk about the little genius type.

There are always movies or books about a genius who could do anything he or she wanted to do. And, because this person is a genius, everyone just treated him or her with kid gloves. The reality is different. Most genius types don't get far in the workplace because their intelligence — impressive though it may be — often fails to produce the kind of common sense solutions needed in today's workplace.

Many times a genius type walks into the workplace fully expecting to be treated with deference, only to get a rude awakening. There are a few times and places where they get the special treatment they want and expect, but here again this is the exception more than the rule. From my observations, I can tell you that how well you did in school doesn't necessarily translate into how well you will do in the workplace.

The New York Times recently reported on an interesting study done by the *Harvard Business Review* at AT&T-Bell Laboratories in New Jersey. According to the research, interpersonal skills play a larger role in success than does intelligence. The study showed that when more personable people needed help, they were more likely to receive the assistance they needed than were their less personable peers.

This revelation is not hard to believe, but nevertheless people in the workplace can sometimes loose track of how important it is to simply "get along" with one's peers.

Here's another example from the world of movies: Have you ever been involved with the take-charge, tell-everyone-else-what-to-do type? These are the people you see publicly embarrassing subordinates and peers. They feel perfectly justified in their approach to people management, because, after all, they know exactly what they're doing and they get the job done. And besides, this sort of personality looks good on the screen. We all have a natural tendency to relate to the lead character as we watch. However, in real life, not only will anyone with such an abrasive personality have problems keeping good subordinates, the take-charge, tell-everyone-else-what-to-do type isn't someone his or her peers will go out of their way to help.

Other unfortunate influences on your style may be summed up by these well-known old sayings: *"Speak softly and carry a big stick,"* and *"Empty wagons make a big noise."*

Both sayings have their merits, but in the workplace, speaking softly may not cut it. You have to let people know you're around. You have to speak up because, as I said earlier, if you don't speak up your colleagues will assume that you don't know what's going on. Besides, how many of us really get to "carry a big stick" in the workplace?

"Empty wagons make a big noise," which indicates that silence has substance, can also promote a dangerous workplace attitude.

As you can see, old adages can encourage you to develop a style which is contrary to the kind of skills you need in the workplace.

I'd also like you to look at your school's role in leading you to form unproductive attitudes and self images.

School is probably one of the worst places in the world when it comes to preparing you for the dynamics of the workplace. This is especially true of college! I say this because it makes almost no difference what you did in school as long as you made good grades. School is an artificial environment, free of the cause-and-effect consequences you will encounter once you leave the ivy-covered campus. As a student, you were free to do almost anything you wanted to do. You could treat (or mistreat) your classmates almost any way you wanted. You didn't have to worry about dealing with different personalities, as long as you made good grades. You learn the system and, past buttering up the occasional professor, you don't really have to take the feelings of your colleagues or your image into consideration.

None of this prepares you for the workplace!

Don't take this as a blanket condemnation of every school in America. What I'm saying is that for the most part schools don't address the human dynamics issues discussed in this book. There are exceptions, thank goodness. I have had people in my seminars describe programs their colleges had developed to expose students to the problems inherent in group efforts. Such programs are truly helpful, but believe me, these schools or programs don't represent the majority in our education system.

Almost everything in school from grade school through a doctorate program is individually based. As a result, students are not prepared for the human dynamics of the workplace. As a result, many people resist making changes to their style simply because the reluctance to do so has become ingrained in their subconscious. This makes it difficult for them to recognize the benefits of being able to change their workplace style to fit individual situations.

ASK YOURSELF THESE STYLE QUESTIONS

You may find yourself reluctant to make the style changes that are requested of you by your manager. The following questions may help you understand, accept and benefit from management feedback:

1. **Is my manager asking me to compromise my values or just to change my behavior?** Make sure you're not confusing a mere request for a behavior change with a change in your moral code or values.
2. **Does it really matter if I disagree with the approach my management is asking me to take?** Keep in mind that it doesn't necessarily matter if the approach you're being asked to take is right or wrong. You're being paid to do it, so go ahead and do it and be through with it. It's not worth the hassle. It's not worth getting your management upset because you're holding out for the way you think things should be done. If management, for some reason, wants things done a certain way, and you don't agree, simply make your observations in a diplomatic fashion, and then get on with the task you're being paid to do. You've gone on record with your objections. Now it's time to put all your energy into doing it the way your management wants it done. You can complain about it at home, if you absolutely must. Don't, however, complain about it at work.

A woman from a past seminar gave a good example.

She told how some of her co-workers were surprised during an informal discussion outside of work that she had disagreed with an approach they were using. This new approach had come down from one of the higher-ups. They were surprised because she had been so positive and supportive of the approach at work.

Her style reflected what we've been talking about here.

She voiced her initial concerns about the approach, but when they were ignored or not considered she said to herself, *"Okay, that's the end of it. I'll support the direction the company wants to go in."*

She felt no need to spread the poison of dissent among the people working with her. Why should she? What would taking a negative stance accomplish? Certainly nothing positive for her individually, and she had already discovered her opinion on the matter would not sway management.

Remember: If you get negative and start criticizing what management is trying to do, you're putting yourself in a precarious position ... and for what?

Also consider this possibility: Just because you disagree doesn't necessarily mean the approach is wrong. There may be a "big picture" reason why things have to be implemented a certain way. The key here is that management holds the controlling position. It really doesn't matter if you are wrong or if your management is wrong. For all practical purposes, the fact that they insist on doing it their way and the fact that you work for them combine to make it the "right way." Certainly it becomes the way you should do it. Think of yourself as a team player and support whatever has to be done.

As another seminar participant put it, many times if you can show your management that you are a team player and you're a supportive and loyal employee, you will be able to find, within the political structure, an avenue to have your concerns heard. In essence, you can still remain very individual and show your creativity within the confines of the structure already in place.

Food for thought: if you were the head of your own company, wouldn't you want employees to do things your way?

3. **Does making this change, change me?** If your basic moral values aren't involved, a style change certainly doesn't change who you are in any fundamental way.

Chapter 9:
Six Ways to Improve Your Style

Now that we've discussed the importance of a good personal work style, let's take a look at six ways you can improve your style. Follow these suggestions and your chances of moving up in your company will increase dramatically.

1. Keep your emotions in check.
2. Utilize the style uniform concept.
3. Seek feedback from your management.
4. Seek out a "sounding board."
5. Observe what's going on around you.
6. Understand your boss's style.

As we examine each of these suggestions separately, try to focus on the changes you will need to make within yourself to improve your style. And remember that these are merely changes to your workplace style, they are not intended to alter your moral outlook or erode your ethics.

1. KEEP YOUR EMOTIONS IN CHECK

This message was delivered to me forcefully several years ago during a discussion with my boss. We were talking about some things that had happened recently. I was extremely irritated at one of my colleagues for what I considered a condescending, disrespectful comment. At one point I asked my boss, *"Do I have "stupid" written across my face?"* He responded by asking me, *"Why are you taking this thing so personally?"* After we talked through my concerns, I realized that what had happened hadn't been directed at me at all. **I was simply taking things too personally.**

Keep in mind that your job is just that ... a job!

I know that you cannot always be totally unemotional and I also know that for many people, a job is more than a job. The trick here is to be circumspect. Let things happen without taking them personally. React to the flow of events, not the personalities involved. Individual actions and situations tend to be related to a position and not a person. In other words, lighten up. The things that happen to you would happen to anyone in your position. It's not you ... it's the job!

2. UTILIZE THE STYLE UNIFORM CONCEPT

Let's talk about a concept I call the **style uniform.**

Your style uniform defines your behavior while you're at work. It separates your personality from "how you do your job." You put it on when you get to work and you take it off when you leave. You don't have to purchase anything. It's invisible to other people, so you don't have to worry about color coordinating your outfits. It's very comfortable. You define it and can change it as you please. The only effect or noticeable difference it has on you is that your behavior, while you're at work, is different from your behavior when you are not at work.

The funny thing about this style uniform is that while you have it on you do the following:

- You interact with other people rationally.
- You're cool under fire.
- You actually listen to what other people have to say.
- You're courteous and you treat other people with respect.
- You don't just complain. You offer suggestions for problems.
- You're a team player.

Basically, you communicate and interact with a style that is accepted and valued in your workplace.

The nice thing about your style uniform is that when you leave work, you can take it off and become your old self again. The things that define you at work don't have to be the things that define you elsewhere. The parts of your style uniform with which you are not particularly comfortable can be removed once you leave work. The moment you walk out the door, you just take that style uniform off and you can, if you wish, become your old self again. My advice: utilize the style uniform; play your role, and when you leave work, take it off.

Of course, if you've done a truly thorough job of building your style uniform, you may find that it is quite useful even away from work.

Challenge Your Thinking Pattern

Alisa Speese is a Staff Director for McDonald's Corporation. As a person heavily involved in people management, she is a savvy observer of the corporate life.

"Roland Nolen's philosophy pulls the covers back and gives people a glimpse into what management is thinking. I believe Roland's concepts challenge the traditional thinking that people have about how they can move ahead. Many people think that their technical performance is enough to move them ahead in their jobs. Roland really builds a good case for saying that you need to be technically competent, but you need so many other things in addition to that.

"A manager should be able to give you feedback about things other than work products and deliverables — things relating to your style and how you interact with others and what kind of a team player you are — these things are critical to your moving ahead.

"Roland's advice to wear your style as your uniform and understand that your style is not tied closely to your moral values is an eye-opener.

"To do your job and carry out the decisions management has made whether or not you agree with those decisions, is a way to really contribute and add value. I know that there are people who have walked into situations and thought 'WOW, this guy doesn't like me because I'm x, y, z' — it could be because you are a woman or because you are a minority, but if you really dig under the covers and look at it, it almost always comes up to what I would term a style issue — where you just have differing ways of communicating, your backgrounds bring different dimensions into your work relationships. If you can get on board with a more open style and start having more open views about the way you operate, that's really the key to success."

3. SEEK FEEDBACK FROM YOUR MANAGEMENT

In just about every seminar I've lead, there will be at least one very earnest person who approaches me and says something like this: *"You've told us how perception problems can get created and how I may have style problems, and I guess I agree with you. But what if I do? What do I do now? How can I correct the situation?"*

Here is my answer: First of all, go to your manager and ask for frank and honest feedback. Ask your manager if he or she views you as having any perception or style problems.

This question is so common that I developed what I call **style worksheets.** (appendix I). These guides should probably be called image and style worksheets, since they address both image and style issues. The worksheets are designed to provide you with a mechanism that will guide you in discussions between you and your manager.

A NOTE OF CAUTION: After attending my seminar, listening to the seminar tape and/or reading this book you may feel passionately that you are completely open to honest feedback. Your manager, however, may still not feel comfortable giving you that feedback. As a result, you may not be completely satisfied with the feedback you receive.

Don't be discouraged. Use the worksheets. They provide, if nothing else, a good starting point.

Here's something to think about when using the worksheets. You may not get anything that comes close to being negative. Everything may be portrayed as totally rosy. Don't be taken in. This may well be an indicator that no matter what you do your manager is not willing to share with you the kind of feedback you need to improve. That may be the point at which you need to move on.

Essentially, if you're not getting honest feedback, you're not in a good situation.

Another cautionary note comes from a recent seminar participant who pointed out that the worksheets should be used at the beginning of the performance review year. She had a friend who used them at performance review time and they worked against her by bringing up negative things her manager had forgotten.

4. SEEK OUT "SOUNDING BOARDS"

One of the most valuable things you can have as a career-related resource is a friend off whom you can bounce ideas and impressions. Since management often has limited opportunities to see you in action, a sympathetic peer may give you better information. The key is to find someone you feel you can trust.

Once you find a confidante, ask him or her questions like these:

- What do you think of my communication skills?
- What do you think of my interpersonal skills?
- How do I handle myself in meetings?

One thing you should keep in mind is the comfort level of the person you ask to help you. This person must believe that you are willing to actually hear the truth. Don't underestimate how hard it is for someone to give a friend honest feedback. People are very uncomfortable giving their honest opinions. They may not want to hurt your feelings or they may have had experiences in the past where giving their honest opinion caused some pain. Put yourself in their position. How would you feel?

5. OBSERVE WHAT IS GOING ON AROUND YOU

Please realize that no single seminar or book is going to tell you everything that's happening in your workplace.

My advice is to watch the successful people around you. The chance to observe and learn from your colleagues is, in my opinion, one of the most under-utilized opportunities in the workplace. This is doubly unfortunate because it's not that hard to do. Observe their style. Listen to their words. Talk to them and ask for their advice. See what I mean? Not really that tough, is it?

One thing you have to do, though, is get **jealousy** out of the equation. This unattractive emotion is one of the major obstacles to learning from successful people. Jealousy will cloud your opinions and prevent you from learning everything there is to learn. Be able to admit it if you like someone's style. I have peers whose style I just love. They're utterly smooth. I try to note the things that they do and put their techniques to work for me.

If you doubt the value of learning from others, take a few moments to observe how many very successful people often ask their peers for advice.

Remember, in all of this you must be **honest** with yourself. Don't try to fool yourself or anyone else. Make an honest assessment.

6. STUDY YOUR BOSS'S STYLE

Take a little time to study your own style. Now make a similar examination of your boss's style

Do they conflict?

For example, if you have a manager who is extremely detail oriented or is obsessed with employee punctuality, you better make sure that you're falling in line. Likewise, if your manager is very organized and notices in certain situations that you are very unorganized, a negative perception will definitely be created.

As human beings, we tend to evaluate employees and colleagues according to our own "yardstick." In other words, we tend to like people who think and act the same way we do. For example, if I believe in being totally organized and I walk into your office where chaos reigns ... I'm going to be reaching some negative conclusions.

Individual personality types heavily influence style. Some people may be more analytical. Others may be more controlling and assertive. For a more comprehensive discussion on how personality and style relate, refer to texts such as Tony Alessandra's *The Platinum Rule* and Roger Dawson's *Secrets of Power Negotiating.* I also suggest that you obtain a self-test booklet from Personal Strengths Publishing (see recommended resources and recommended reading at the end of this book).

William J. Skeens of Lucent Technologies gives this advice: *Understand your own strengths and interests and find a manager who will value them.* Here are some of his practical suggestions:

Seek out a job that plays to your strengths. If you are in a job that emphasizes your weaknesses ... get out.

Ask yourself, "What do I value?" It doesn't matter if you are big on individual contributions or think that teamwork is more effective. The important thing is that you find a manager who has the same values.

CLOSING OBSERVATIONS ON STYLE

Over several years of working on workplace style with seminar attendees I have come to a couple of important conclusions. These observations are nearly universal in all working situations:

Becoming an extrovert is half the battle when it comes to changing your style. Introverts with their inherently quiet personalities have a tough, even painful, time improving their style. Being an introvert myself, I can tell you that sharing one's thoughts and opinions in various forums and being willing to "mingle" are contrary to an introvert's basic psychological blueprint.

I once received the following feedback from a seminar participant: "It seems to me that you want us to have multiple personalities ... what about integrity?"

Yes, I do want you to have "multiple personalities," but in a positive sense. Do I want you to act and carry yourself one way in the workplace and possibly a different way (more of your usual self) when you are not at work? YES! Does that require you to lose your integrity? I definitely don't think so. In essence, the purpose of this whole style discussion is to get you to see that many of the changes management may ask you to make are simply changes to your workplace behavior.

As trite as it may sound, people like to work with pleasant people. While I was writing this book, I spent a lot of time trying to encapsulate what I meant by good style. I realized that if you have a good attitude and style you are probably also someone who is pleasant to work with.

As we continue to build our definition of "working smart," we'll build upon the two components we've discussed so far:

WORKING SMART

- Manage Your Image (Perceptions)
- Improve Your Style

Chapter 10:

A New Perspective for Minorities and Women

In some workplaces, if you're a minority or a woman, racism and sexism can become genuine obstacles to your success. The degree to which these prejudices affect your career may vary from one workplace to another, and not every workplace has a problem. However, to ignore these factors and pretend that they do not exist would do a grave disservice to anyone who reads this book.

I am not, however, going to address, in general, the issues of racism and sexism in these pages. Dealing with those concerns in any workplace necessitates a commitment from management and would require numerous, carefully planned seminars and workshops. Instead, I am going to deal with things you can control, things that can help you become more positive and productive. As Stephen Covey (author of *The 7 Habits of Highly Effective People*) would say, I want you to concentrate on things that are in your "sphere of influence."

If you're a minority or a woman, I want you to step back and take a new look at your workplace and an honest look at yourself, because it's very easy to misinterpret some management actions as having racist or sexist overtones. Do you have perception problems that might require some personal work? Could your style stand some improving? In other words, I don't want you blaming racism or sexism for your problems, if in fact they had nothing to do with the situation. I have seen it happen. It is easy to blame outside factors and other people for your problems. That is a natural human tendency. That's why I want to make sure that you take an honest look at yourself first.

Once you have done that you will know when other things are coming into play and you will know what action to take.

USE THE "JERK PRINCIPLE"

I used to think that minorities and women had a vastly different set of problems. We don't have natural access to the "good old boy" network and we often don't have natural access to mentors and sponsors. The reality, however, is that not all white males do either! In fact, I'd have to argue that the good-old-boy network represents a very small percentage of people. That is why I say that for the majority of people in the workplace, the problems encountered are nearly universal, no matter what your ethnic background or gender. Most people in the workplace are struggling with perception and style issues.

When you add sexist or racist elements to the problems already common to just about every workplace, the result is like turning up the volume on bad music. It just makes it sound even worse.

My advice for minorities and women is to utilize the *"jerk principle."*

Understand that one of the main things that may be hindering you is your societal conditioning. We all deal, at one time or another, with people who do have hang-ups regarding race or gender. After a while you begin to recognize the tone and circumstances that often lead to confrontations with prejudiced and bigoted colleagues or customers. That is conditioning.

Our conditioning can lead us to assume the worst in a given situation.

To avoid that unpleasant and unproductive frame of mind, I suggest that you utilize the "jerk principle." Here is an example: Imagine that you've gone to see John because you need some information from him. If he is uncooperative or downright rude, your conditioning as a minority may make you interpret his rudeness as "racist behavior." But remember that **it is very difficult to tell the difference between a jerk and a racist.**

Similarly, it's very hard to tell the difference between a sexist and a jerk if you're a female working with insensitive people. **The jerk principle basically says, do not personalize the situ-**

ation. Just say to yourself, *"This a jerk. I know if someone else had walked in, this jerk would have acted the same way with that person."* The odds are that the apparent racist or sexist action or remark is the result of unsolved style problems.

But if you personalize the situation, what happens? Your whole approach to the problem is different. That is, when you view someone as being a racist or sexist, your whole thought process takes on a much more negative flavor.

You don't want to deal with sexists and racists. You don't want to have anything to do with them. When you utilize the "jerk principle," you start figuring out ways to make the jerk give you the information you need. This moves you into a completely different thought process. You're not spending time worrying about racist or sexist behavior, which is good because such negative brain activity can drain your energy. When you're working to solve the problems presented by a jerk, however, you don't have to take things personally. You can just write them off and you go on about your business: no more negative thoughts. You deal with the situation in a more business-like fashion.

The key to this level of success and accomplishment is your ability to avoid personalizing the incident or situation.

I used to say utilize the jerk principle until you could determine exactly what the other person's problem was. I have amended that position. Why put the other person's attitude under a microscope. What does it matter if he/she is a racist or just a jerk. What can you do about it? Why bother? Go about doing what you have to do. I would advise you, when you run into these difficult situations with people, to view the problem person as a jerk and protect yourself. You're not going to be able to change someone's long-held prejudices in the short term anyway. Don't waste your time and energy. Concentrate instead on being as productive as possible.

Look at it this way: even if the person was indeed a sexist or racist, you still have to work with them to get your job done. If you don't find some way to deal with them effectively your performance will suffer. Figure out in advance how you are going to handle these situations.

A past seminar participant gave this advice: you should formalize, as much as possible, your interactions with the person.

Put your relationship in very formal terms that explain what you expect and what the other person can expect. That way it's all on the record. You will still have to interact with the person, but by formalizing the relationship you protect yourself in case you don't get the cooperation or the information you need.

Please understand that when I say there is nothing you can do, I'm not talking about harassment! When these unpleasant situations occur, you should always notify your management as soon as possible and keep a record of all such incidents. I have heard people say *"I don't want to involve my management, because it could hurt the working relationship."*

Believe me, **you don't have a working relationship** with anyone who harasses you in any way!

USE SOCIAL EVENTS AND INTERACTIONS TO YOUR ADVANTAGE

Often, minorities and women tend to feel isolated in the workplace. As a result, attending social events or interacting with colleagues can make them feel uncomfortable. If that's the case with you, don't let your lack of comfort get in the way of your success. Those events and interactions are valuable because they represent opportunities for people to get to know you.

I contend that people base many of their opinions about you on how much they have in common with you. Have you ever been on a business trip or taken a workshop with someone with whom you felt you had very little in common? Then, after the trip or course, you found yourself with a completely altered view of that person because you had gotten to know them better.

If you're a minority or woman, you're already viewed by some of your colleagues as different. Thus, you have more to overcome before your manager and peers will begin to "relate" to you in a positive fashion. If you avoid social interactions, how can someone get to know you? You may even be viewed as unsociable or suspicious. Social and personal interactions help you establish rapport with people. You need that rapport, because, as a minority or woman, you already have enough obstacles. There is no reason to add to them.

You should, therefore, view these social events and interactions as **opportunities to relate.**

A friend of mine gave this example: He was at a social function, seated near a middle level manager from his company. His only thought at the time was that he should talk about work, his way of showing his dedication. He noticed, however, after a few minutes that he was no longer a part of the conversation. He was honest enough with himself to admit that his exclusion from the conversation wasn't because of his race. It was because one of his peers had started talking about a play that the manager was interested in seeing.

Social events and interactions are also excellent opportunities for networking, if you will excuse the rather shopworn buzzword.

At the root, networking is nothing more than the search for rapport with people who can help you. For example, I have been in customer meetings that beg the question, *"was it really worth the cost?"* It depends upon your point of view and the mission of the meeting. Maybe nothing tangible was acquired or accomplished, but from the standpoint of establishing rapport with customers, the meetings were definitely worth the cost and effort.

KNOW WHEN TO QUIT AND MOVE ON

Over the years, I have advised several people in bad work situations to either transfer or change jobs.

This is not an easy piece of advice to give, nor is it an easy piece of advice to accept and act upon. However, none of the people involved have regretted making the move.

The crux of the matter is this: if you don't have a supportive manager or environment, you're simply beating your head against a wall. No matter what you do, it won't be good enough. Any manager who is operating from a racist or sexist point of view will never allow you to prove yourself.

I have had friends who thought they could prove things, even to an extremely prejudiced manager, by achieving flawless execution on the job. This, of course, is a fallacy. There is no such thing as flawless execution. We all make mistakes. If your manager is burdened by racist or sexist sensibilities, he or she is merely waiting for you to make a mistake that will "confirm" his or her prejudices. Any good manager knows that we cannot learn without making mistakes. Throughout your career, you will make mistakes and use them to improve your performance.

If your manager doesn't realize the value of mistakes or if his or her prejudice makes a productive working relationship impossible, don't waste your time trying to fix the unfixable. Be scrupulously honest with your self-analysis and don't be afraid to quit and move on to a more promising situation with another employer. Know what you're fighting. Know when to quit.

Chapter 11:

Looking at Yourself From a Manager's Perspective

Ask yourself these questions: If you have a bad working relationship with your manager, whose problem is it? And who has the biggest stake in working the problem out?

Many employees think that their managers should try to understand them. If you share that opinion, you are almost certainly in for a rude awakening. It's up to you to craft a mutually workable relationship with your manager.

As I said earlier, studies have shown that the number one source of job stress and frustration is your immediate manager. That fact, alone, demonstrates why it is so important that you understand your manager's perspective. Here are some questions I have asked in my seminars:

- **Do you feel you get enough feedback from your manager?** On the average, about 70% of the people said, *"No, I don't get enough feedback."*
- **Do you get negative as well as positive feedback?** Most people said they received specific, negative feedback and about 50% said they could improve based on the feedback they were getting.
- **Do you think your boss is telling you the "whole truth?"** 74% percent of the people said they did not believe they were being told the "whole truth."

I think the messages here are very clear: People want more feedback from their managers, and people don't necessarily trust what their managers are telling them!

WHY MANAGERS DON'T ALWAYS TELL YOU THE WHOLE TRUTH

There is an excellent chance that your manager does not tell you the whole, unadulterated truth when he or she talks to you about your performance.

Before we go any further, however, let me state most emphatically that I don't for a moment think that there is any kind of conspiracy (global or otherwise) on management's part to intentionally deceive you or to withhold valuable information from you or your colleagues. If you are not being told the whole truth and nothing but the truth, the problem can probably be traced to the fact that managers are human.

A quick study of human nature reveals some perfectly logical, if misguided, reasons why managers don't tell you the whole truth.

First, many managers don't want to de-motivate people. They honestly believe that if the feedback they give you is too honest, harsh, or negative, they will kill your desire to work hard and do a good job.

Giving someone completely candid feedback is a risky business. While just about everyone will tell you that they want "honest feedback," they don't always react in a constructive fashion. As a result, you will see managers trying to soften the impact of their criticism. Managers have a job to do. They want to make sure that the job gets done. Their livelihood depends on people getting the job done. The last thing they want to do is de-motivate people and make the job harder to get done.

Also, some managers simply don't want to deal with personnel issues. They probably shouldn't be managers, because they really don't like the personnel aspect of the job. They are usually very good at some other aspect of their work ... perhaps the technical, non-people part. They may view personnel issues as an unfortunate, unwanted duty that comes with the job. They dread performance or merit evaluation time.

Additionally, some people are simply afraid to have disagreements or confrontations. It's easy to see that if a manager dreads that sort of interaction they may not be willing to be totally honest with people. To avoid an unpleasant situation, they may filter what they tell you.

Here's an example from a management workshop I attended: we were grouped in teams and everyone was given different roles to play as managers and employees. We were role-playing in fictional performance evaluation discussions. During the recap, one of the team leaders reported how one of the managers waited 20 minutes before he said anything negative to the person who was going to be fired. If that manager had problems giving the right feedback during role playing, how do you think he would handle giving negative feedback to someone in real life?

In all fairness, however, if you think it's tough on the employee side of the table during performance discussions, consider the view from the manager's side. Managers are sitting there worried about de-motivating people or having confrontations. It's never pleasant to deliver criticism, especially if the other person loses his or her emotional grip during the discussion. Employees may get very upset and some may cry. I'm sure you've heard of some cases where things can really get ugly and dangerous … disgruntled employees returning with automatic weapons and that sort of thing.

Fortunately, it doesn't always have to be that way. A friend of mine who once worked for a huge multi-national publishing company as an in-house freelancer told me this story: *"I was working in a division of the company that had some less-than-impressive performance numbers. I knew that my future as a freelancer attached to the company was uncertain at best. I also suspected that they were about to shut down the whole division. It turned out that I was right.*

"During the week, I saw a lot of people go into the manager's office and emerge five minutes later with tears in their eyes. A couple of them really dug into the manager and threatened lawsuits and all sorts of trouble. So, when it came to my turn, I walked into the manager's office and told him, 'George, I know you called me in here to fire me and I just want to tell you that I understand. I appreciate the work you've given me so far and I hope we'll be able to get together on another project in the future. You've been a great boss and I'll miss working for you. I know that

a nice guy like you probably has a hard time letting people go, but don't worry about me. I have lots of contacts and resources and I'll land on my feet.' He just sat there for a minute staring at me. Then he asked me to sit down for a minute. Told me he appreciated everything I said and if he ever had another freelance position open with the company he would call me first. It was a nice moment for both of us. Of course, I was still out of work. I did get a great reference from him, though. I actually did think he was a nice guy, although I would have said and done the same thing no matter what I thought about him. No sense burning any bridges."

Here's yet another reason why managers are not always completely candid: some people simply refuse to listen. They don't really want genuine feedback, even thought they may say that they do. Often they will refuse to accept negative criticism or they will blow the criticism way out of proportion.

The major problem that hinders many people from accepting negative feedback is that they get too hung up on "facts," as opposed to perception. These people get so busy defending themselves that they actually end up worse off than they were at the beginning of the feedback session. And here's a bitter irony: they may be right about the "facts." The manager may be using faulty information to make his or her judgements. That, however, does not really matter. What matters is your reaction to the situation. When you react too emotionally or refuse to listen, you'll be beating yourself two ways. First, you'll never get an opportunity to understand how your manager arrived at his or her perception. And it's that process of forming perceptions that is all-important to your advancement. Two, you'll brand yourself as an unreasonable, overemotional employee whose attitude makes a working relationship difficult. You don't want either of those things to happen. Trust me on this.

I can guarantee you that once a manager forms the perception that you're not going to listen, he is certainly not going to bother trying to tell you anything remotely useful.

Imagine the following scenario (taken from my own experience): during a performance evaluation discussion, a group of managers had some negative feedback they felt they had to give to one of their employees. The employee's immediate manager said, *"This is one of the few people in my group I can give this kind of feedback to."*

That statement said volumes about the other employees in that manager's group. They were not getting the feedback they needed to improve, because they had already let their manager know that they were not willing to listen. I'm sure that the person willing to accept the negative feedback is going a good deal farther than his less receptive peers.

Of course, the fault is not always with the employees being evaluated. Some managers like to take the "I'm the boss" stance. They feel that performance evaluation discussion is the time for them to tell you what they think and you're only supposed to meekly listen as they "straighten you out." These god-like individuals are certain that they know what's best for you. It's very hard for these managers to separate the facts from the perceptions. It's also very easy for this kind of manager to offend an employee during evaluation.

Lastly, managers may not tell employees the whole truth, because after a point they may make "automatic" judgments based on their long-held perceptions of a given employee. These opinions get filed away in their minds and almost everything that employee does after that point is filtered through that "file." By this time, a manager in this mode of thinking has also decided whether he likes you. His opinions become almost subconscious and he will start judging you based solely on those opinions. As a result, you could be doing great work, but not getting fully recognized for it because of these pre-formed opinions. What makes this problem so tough to address is that these opinions may have become so subconscious that the manager may not even realize that he has them.

WHAT YOU REALLY DID WRONG

About the worst thing you can do to your manager (and to your own career) is to **embarrass her in front of her boss.**

Make this one egregious mistake and I can guarantee you that your manager will not forget you. You may never find out just how upset she was, but **she will pay you back.** She will remember the incident forever and it will overshadow everything you do from that point. I am not saying that all managers will be openly vindictive (although a small percentage might), but what I am saying is that the embarrassment will influence your manager's opinion of you and determine the kinds of assignments and responsibilities he or she will give you. The greater the embarrassment, the more damage your career will sustain.

There are a number of ways you can embarrass your manager. One of the worst ways is to make him look bad in front of his boss and his peers … especially if the contradiction or remark takes place in some public forum or company meeting.

You can also hurt your manager by not keeping him informed, or by "taking your sweet time" getting status information to him. Then, when his boss asks for a status report, he can't come up with it. This is very embarrassing for him and very dangerous for you.

Another serious mistake is to let your manager down when she is depending heavily on you. For example, let's say that I walk into your office and say, *"I need this task done by Friday."* You don't want to look bad, so you say, *"Okay, Roland, I'll take care of it."* That assignment does not come from me alone. My own boss expects me to report back on Friday. Actually, it came down from my boss's boss. You tell me you'll take care of it and everything will be fine. By the way, today is Monday. Then here comes Friday. It's about ten o'clock in the morning and I'm starting to get a little nervous. I haven't heard from you. Where's the information I need from you? Now it's getting close to noon and I'm getting real nervous. I finally find you, and you say, *"Oh, I didn't get a chance to do that. I had to do these other things and I just didn't get a chance to do your project. I'm sorry."*

This immediately sets off a daisy chain of disappointment and embarrassment. I have to go back to my boss and say, *"I don't have the information you needed."* My boss then has to go back to his boss and confess that he doesn't have it. My boss is not going to forget me, because I didn't get the job done. His boss is not going to forget him, because he didn't get his job done. Excuses don't matter. What matters is that the job didn't get done.

I can guarantee you that **I'll never depend on you again** for anything important. And that's the good news! There are managers out there who would take a more personal, vengeful point of view. They may even intentionally do something to hurt your career. But even if your manager doesn't go that far, you are still damaged goods in his eyes. Once a manager puts you into that category, you are definitely not going to be considered one of their Top Performers.

Understand, as a manager, I won't care what you were doing that caused you to fail at the task I had given you. You may have a very good excuse. Maybe it was something very important. You may have actually made a decent priority call, but I simply won't care. You embarrassed me in front of my boss. Unfortunately, you could work yourself to death after that point and I won't care. All I'll remember is that you let me down and caused me to be embarrassed.

A seminar participant once asked me, *"Are you saying that once you messed up so bad you might as well look for another job because as far as your manager is concerned you will never be a Top Performer?"*

That was exactly what I was saying ... if the embarrassment was great enough.

Some friends of mine, a married couple, were in that same session. After the session the wife said that she didn't think anyone could really embarrass their boss bad enough to cause them to have to change jobs. Her husband commented that he believed it could happen, because just recently at his company a manager had been fired and the rumor mill said it was because he had made some inappropriate comments at a high-level meeting.

Naturally, not all interactions between managers and employees are as dramatic as the examples I've mentioned. Not every incident is a potential job-killer. Usually when you embarrass your boss it's over something in what could be called a gray area. Maybe you let the boss down, but you didn't cause severe enough embarrassment to make him abandon you completely. If "the chain of embarrassment" isn't there you will have a much better chance to recover. When some sort of employee-inspired embarrassment has happened to me (and, trust me, it has) my feedback to them was, "let me make the priority calls."

If you agree to do something for me and then a conflict occurs, let me know and I'll make the priority call. Always let your manager make the priority call (Is the task scheduled to be completed on Friday important enough for you to ignore other work conflicts?).

What usually happens, however, is that people will independently make the priority calls. Sometimes they make the right call, other times they don't. Some managers will tell you, *"You let me down and I'm disappointed."* I have told people, *"You let me down,"* and warned them that *"if something like this happens again, I won't care about all the other work you have done."*

The real danger is when you have a manager who won't tell you how much you have let him down. He'll just quietly fume and say to himself, *"I'm not going to depend on that guy anymore."* When you go through performance evaluation with that kind of manager you will usually find very vague feedback, because he won't come out and say what it was that disappointed him. Also, since he will no longer depend on you for important jobs, you will be viewed as no more than an average performer. You will probably become frustrated because you won't be able to figure out why you're not getting credit for all the great, hard work you're doing. Your hard work will have become seriously devalued. As far as your manager is concerned, you're a good hard worker, but you're not a "best performer."

Making a good impression on your manager also has to do with how you interact with your peers.

Often, a manager will observe your dealings with your peers and draw certain conclusions about you. For example, if you are abrasive with your peers, management will notice or hear about it. You will be categorized as being abrasive and not very good at working with other people. You may or may not be told that this is one of your problems. There could also be things that you did or said in the course of the working day that just turned your manager off.

You have to watch what you say and do.

I heard one manager put it this way: "You're stupid if you think we don't judge everything we see you say and do, regardless of whether it's at work or at a work-related social event. If you're thinking about letting your hair down at a company party, don't. Managers have a very human tendency to subconsciously record everything they hear and see their employees doing. I don't care how informal the conversation, your manager is recording and remembering it all."

Let me emphasize this point further. A manager once told me he wouldn't promote a person who worked for him because of the way the person acted when playing golf. He felt the person's childish behavior and temper tantrums on the golf course revealed a basically flawed personality that would eventually manifest itself in the workplace. He therefore felt the person would not make a good manager. As you can see, playing golf with the right people isn't always a guarantee of success.

Another potential source of damaging feedback is your peer group at work. Unfortunately, they, too, will often fail to tell you the whole truth about their perspective on your performance. That, however, does not mean that they won't tell somebody else what they think. You would be amazed at how many enlightening workplace conversations take place behind closed doors. You could be the star topic in one of these impromptu evaluation sessions and not even know it. Nor will you have, in such cases, any opportunity to defend yourself. You're lucky to even hear about them.

How does this sort of unfortunate back-stabbing happen? The most common way is when the Star Performer or the right hand person talks about you to the manager. Do you think that the manager will go back and verify whether the damning testimony is accurate? It's not likely. The manager's view is *"Why should I? My Star Performer told me John's a jerk. So why am I going to question that? I don't have to bother. My Star Performer gave me all the information I need."*

You will never know.

WHAT DOES A MANAGER LIKE TO SEE?

George Williams looks up from the e-mail his 8-year-old son has just sent him and sees James Thomas peering through his office door.

"Hi, George, got a few minutes to help out an old buddy?"

"Sure," George replies. "You're not selling those candy bars for your daughter's dance troupe again are you?"

"No," James says with a laugh, "nothing like that. I just thought you might be able help me out with a quick, guru-like answer."

"Okay," George says, pushing his keyboard back under his computer. "What can I do for you, James?"

"You know Jeannie Mason, don't you?"

George nods. "What about her? She's not selling candy bars, is she?"

"She's worked for me for about eight months now," Jim explains. "Today she cornered me and wanted to know what it took to be a Top Performer in my division. It was weird, but I couldn't really tell her. I'm embarrassed to admit it, but I mumbled something about how she had to have good communication skills, have good people skills, and do a good job."

"That's true," George says, leaning back in his chair and gazing briefly out at the parking lot where the five o'clock traffic is beginning to thin out. "She needs to have all those things going for her."

"Sure, but then she countered by saying she was good at all those things, and yet she didn't think she was considered a Top Performer. I couldn't succinctly tell her why, so then I start telling her something like she wasn't an expert like Jon. I could tell she wasn't buying it and to be honest with you, I wouldn't either if I were her."

"What did you do?"

"I finally just told her to give me a little time to think about it some more and I would get back to her. I know that you would have had a much better answer. So tell me, guru, what would you have told her? What do you think it takes to become a Top Performer around here?"

George pushes his chair back from his desk and stands up. *"You know where you got in trouble, don't you?"* he says, grinning at James.

A look of confusion flashes across James' face as he straightens his tie and joins George at the south window.

"What do you mean?"

George squints in the bright sunlight and explains.

"She wanted you to give her a checklist that would define a Top Performer so she could simply go down the list checking what she has done and anything that wasn't checked she could work on it. From her perspective, she felt that you should have been able to produce a list of things she needed to do to become a Top Performer. When you couldn't give her that magic list, then she felt she must be a Top Performer ... just as a matter of definition."

"You're right," says James, waving an arm and knocking over a small pencil holder on George's desk.

"I was sitting there feeling this pressure to produce a checklist and part of me felt I should have been able to, but another part was saying it's not that simple."

George helps his friend pick up the half dozen pencils that have rolled under his desk.

"This is where a lot of confusion and misunderstanding between employees and managers takes place," he explains, *"because employees think we should be able to generate this simple checklist. It's a real human thing to want that list, but we know that there are a lot of dynamics involved when you're trying to get management to recognize you as a Top Performer. You have to*

polish your interpersonal and communication skills, your attitude, your ability to work with others. And, most importantly, you have to realize that you're not dealing with a totally objective process. No matter how hard we may try as managers to make objective evaluations, you and I know how subjective this stuff gets."

"Is that what you tell your employees?" James asks looking a little perplexed.

"Well, I start by telling people that the performance process can get very subjective and there is not a magic checklist. But I can tell them the things that I as well as other managers like to see and what we value the most in an employee."

"Go ahead," says James, as he prepares to take notes.

"First, I ask them to think about the work-related things we value as the layers used in building a pyramid. At the base, they have to dependable, reliable, and responsive. I try to get them to see that I have to be able to depend on them before I can trust them."

"Sounds good so far," James observes. *"Keep going."*

"For example, if I give an employee an assignment, then I should be able to depend on that person to get the job done ... without my having to provide constant reminders, ask for progress reports, and worry about if the job is going to get done right. If an employee of mine is not dependable on small assign-ments, I am certainly not going to trust him or her with a big, im-portant job. Of course, if you never have any of the big assignments, there's no way you will ever be thought of as a Top Performer."

"I see what you mean," James says, *"As a manager, if I can depend on someone to get a job done, no matter how small, then when the big important job comes I know who I can trust to make me look good. There's no way I'm going to risk giving it to some-one who's flaked out on small job.*

"Come to think of it," James continues, *"I have to check up on Jean sometimes. Not like Terri Johnson. I just give her the as-signment and I never worry about it again. I know Terri will get the thing done on schedule ... or maybe even ahead of schedule. And if she has a problem, she lets me know about it right away, while there's still a chance I can do something about it. She doesn't wait until the last minute like a lot of other employees."*

"*Sounds like you're answering your own question, James,*" George says. "*I always try to make people understand that having friends in high places only works if you are also doing a great job and building a good workplace image. I mean, if you're my friend, but you're not dependable or responsive, I'm not going to let you have an opportunity to make me look bad. That's where friendship ends and business begins.*"

"*OK, I understand what you mean by dependable and reliable, but exactly what do you mean by responsive?*"

George thinks a moment and says, "*You know Jane Stewart don't you? Whenever I leave her a message or tell her to stop by and see me, she always makes it a point to get back to me as soon as possible. If she can't for some reason, she lets me know and supplies as much information she can. Sometimes she'll ask me to leave more details so she can get on with the job without talking to me personally. And take those administrative write-ups we're always having to hand in with our projects ... she never misses a deadline or forgets to turn them in.*

"*I have a ton of people in my group who are always forgetting the details and causing me headaches. I'm sure you have people in your group like that as well. You see, James, those people think that the small, administrative jobs aren't important. What they don't realize is that by not taking care of the small details, they are forcing us to deal them out of the big projects. Important jobs just cannot be left to people who blow the details. It's as simple as that.*"

"*That makes a lot of sense to me,*" James says.

"*So ... do you think you have enough to straighten things out for Jeannie the next time she comes to you looking for a checklist?*" George asks as a quick smile plays across his face.

"*I think so, Mr. Guru. And if I don't I guess I can always sell her a few of those dance troupe candy bars. Thanks for the help.*"

Learning what managers really like to see can be a difficult task.

Very few managers are as well prepared for the question as was our friend George in the above scenario. In fact, some of us don't really have an easily articulated answer. Maybe it's like art. We can't tell you what we like, but we recognize it when we see it.

I definitely had to stop and think the first time I was asked what I like to see as a manager. It wasn't an easy concept to put into a formula because many of the things we use to judge people are very subjective (although I have to say that the vast majority of managers honestly try to be objective). In fact, many of our judgments are based on almost subconscious evaluations.

So let's take a moment and try to figure out what really separates people for me, as well as for other managers. There are, in my opinion, six major areas. Taken together they form a "success pyramid."

Figure 3: Success Pyramid — What Managers Like to See

Let's take a more comprehensive look at each of these important areas.

DEMONSTRATE YOUR RELIABILITY AND RESPONSIVENESS

I doubt if you can find any effective manager (at any level) who has a "right hand person" who is not dependable. Here's where having "friends in high places" is not enough. Friend or not, for you to be a manager's right hand person, you have to be reliable and responsive. Those are the same qualities you will have to cultivate if you wish to be a Top Performer. You have to deliver on promised work ... no matter how small. If you're unable to deliver on time, you have to inform your manager early. Don't wait until something is due (or past due) and then spring the bad news on him.

When I say you must be responsive I mean that you should act quickly on a manager's request. Don't wait for a manager to remind you. Get on it right away! These are the kinds of things that define how dependable and responsive you are.

If I give you a task and I don't have to think about it any more because I know you will get the job done, that's my definition of reliable and responsive. I will reward that kind of behavior. Believe me, not every employee is like that.

As a manager, you have to do a lot of checking up on some people. When that happens, the employee in question has immediately painted himself as something less than reliable and responsive.

It is worth asking (as one seminar attendee did) why managers are so hyper about the issue of reliability and responsiveness. Think of it like this: As a manager, what am I trying to do more than anything else? I'm trying to get a lot of quality work produced on time and on budget so that I can move on to the next item and continue to build my own career. In other words, I am trying to impress MY boss. The more items I take care of, the better I look. **The more you help me look good at my job, the more I like you.** It's that simple.

Let's talk about how brief interactions with a manager can influence his or her perception of you. I've been in performance evaluations and heard managers speak very positively about people who didn't work directly for them. The amazing part, though, was that their impressions of these people were often based on brief interactions (sometimes no more than a 15-minute discussion ... out of an entire year!). Talk about the power of perceptions!

How can a manager be so impressed during such a short interaction? My guess is that the manager saw (or sensed) in the employee one or more of the qualities we are discussing right now: responsiveness and reliability.

The manager may have called the person, asked a question and received a prompt, well-thought-out answer. Or maybe the employee went out of her way to help the manager get the answer. At any rate, that interaction set the tone. That person now has someone in management who believes that she is indeed a Star Performer. That's not a bad return for 15 minutes out of an entire year.

Here's another example: One of my colleagues was giving me some performance feedback regarding a person who worked for me. She said that the person let little things drop. On face value that comment would suggest the person probably didn't pay attention to the detail aspects of his job. After getting her to elaborate, I found out the employee in question had scheduled meetings with her and had shown up late several times. Sometimes he didn't even make it to the meetings at all. Worse, he hadn't even called to let her know he was running late. To make things even harder to take, he often failed to give her timely status on some of the things he was doing. When I talked to him about these issues, he had valid reasons for missing the meetings. Usually, he was taking care of some other high priority item and didn't think it was that important for him to be at the meetings on time.

What the preceding example shows is that, to this manager, taking care of those "little things" are how an employee demonstrates his or her reliability and responsiveness. The manager felt that when you scheduled a meeting with her, she should be able to expect you to be there. If you're not going to make it, you need let her know in advance. If you don't provide your manager with status and progress reports, how will she know what's happening? As I said earlier, managers live on status information. The other message here is that you have to delve deeply into the feedback that managers give. Make sure you understand what's really going on. If I had assumed I understood what my colleague meant by "letting little things drop," I would have never found out that the problem really had to do with being dependable and responsive. I would have given the person in my group incorrect feedback.

The unfortunate part of this example is that the employee in question actually had some relatively valid reasons. He was just handling things the wrong way. All he had to do was call the manager and say, *"I can't make the meeting for this reason,"* and the manager probably would have been okay with that. By not making that extra step, the perception was created that he was not responsive or dependable.

Here's an important piece of advice: If you tell a manager, "I'll get back to you today," you had better make sure you deliver on your promise. Even if you don't have the answer, contact the manager and say that you are still working on the issue and don't have an answer yet. Explain that you will contact the manager as soon as you do have the information. This is another case of taking a preventative step to show that you are dependable and that you do what you say you are going to do. If you fail to follow up as promised, the manager may feel that you didn't take his request seriously or that you were just giving him lip service. The point here is that managers will perceive you as unreliable if you don't do what you say you're going to do. A simple concept perhaps, but an important one.

DO WHAT YOUR BOSS THINKS IS IMPORTANT

Not doing what the boss thinks is important is one of the major sources of conflict between managers and the people reporting to them.

This is, in my experience, because people tend to give the top priority to what they like to do. Unfortunately, what you like to do is not necessarily what is the most important.

I had someone come to me and ask me to mediate between him and his manager. He spent about half an hour in my office, telling me about the great work he was doing and how his manager didn't seem to appreciate it. I must admit, the story sounded good and really made me wonder what was going on between him and his manager. When I investigated, the manager jumped all over me with equally convincing stories about all of the things that the employee wasn't doing. That's when I said to myself, *"Roland, what are you doing here? Haven't you had enough of this? You need to get out of the mediation business."* It took me several trips back and forth between the manager and the employee before I could figure out what was happening. Basically, the employee was not doing what his manager felt was the most important work to be done. His manager wanted three documents written ... three lousy documents! What was the person doing? He was doing everything else under the sun. His beeper was going off all the time. He was working hard. He was doing just about everything you could imagine, except writing those three documents.

What was going on in his mind? He didn't want to write those documents, simply because he didn't like to write. His error was in thinking he could impress his manager by doing all this other great work and that would somehow get the emphasis off those

---

Understand What Management Wants

Bob Stanojev is a partner with Ernst & Young's Management Consulting Division.

"It is not important that you work hard — certainly working hard is very important to success — it's that you are working on the right things that add value to the company and that add value to the manager. Sometimes that message never gets clearly communicated to people and that lack of understanding of what the measures are that management is most concerned about is really critical to employees getting recognition, economic rewards and promotions that are available.

"Management is a two-way street. Sometimes the problems that exist are caused by managers not having the ability or insight initially to communicate the things that they think are most important. The priorities that managers have are really set by what the company is trying to achieve in the marketplace and the manager's role is to execute the overall corporate strategy and directives. You, as the employee, need to be aligned with what the executives and managers want to do. If you go off and operate independently and are disconnected from the logical business process, you are doing a disservice to the company first and foremost, a disservice to the manager, and ultimately a tremendous disservice to yourself.

"Roland puts forth a pretty clear picture of what you need to do to be successful in the social environment of the workplace."

"I think every major U.S. corporation that is hiring people into their first-time job market would be well ahead if they would go forth with a program like Roland's.

dreaded documents. He and his manager had been through many discussions about how important those documents were. They had set up several schedules aimed at getting the documents done. Those documents were the most important things to his manager, so all the other work simply didn't matter!

Remember, if you're not doing what your boss thinks is important, you're missing the point.

A similar situation happened to a friend of mine who worked as an editor at a large periodical publishing company in California. My friend supervised several writers, all of whom were required to do a significant amount of research before beginning their writing assignments. One writer, however, never seemed to be able to get into the writing stage. She would constantly find new avenues of information to be explored and new leads that had to be followed up. All of that was perfectly all right with my editor friend … except that all of this meticulous research never generated an article. The writer (or should we say non-writer) simply didn't understand that the company's priority was to write and publish magazine articles. Finally, the writer lost her job. Later, my friend the editor told me that he felt that, had he been a better communicator, he could have made the young woman understand and work on the problem. Unfortunately, that didn't happen … as it often doesn't happen in other manager/employee situations.

Although the above examples are somewhat extreme, they do illustrate a common problem in the workplace: **People are not doing what their boss thinks is important.**

A more typical situation may involve procrastination. You put off an unappealing task simply because it isn't something that you like to do. In the meantime, you do all the other things that you like to do. Usually, it's the administrative or political aspects of the job that people don't like. One way you can solve this problem is to do the unpleasant things first and get them out of the way. When you adopt this plan, two things will happen: You will have avoided that feeling of dread that always accompanies procrastination and your boss will begin to see you as someone who gets things done.

Recently, I read an article on "busy work" in *Entrepreneur* magazine and was amazed when I saw consultants in the training profession discussing the problem of employees not doing what their bosses think is important. There was, the article said, a clear and extremely common mismatch in the workplace between what employees were working on and what their boss thought was important.

One way to mitigate this problem is to avoid getting too emotionally attached to an assignment or job. If your manager changes the priority of a job, don't get hung up on how much time you've already spent on the job. Develop the flexibility to say *"Okay, this job is no longer the number one priority, I'll just switch to the new number one priority and work on it."* Since priority calls are usually driven by business needs, don't take a priority call personally. After all, you're being paid to do whatever task your management says is the most important.

People often don't seem to understand the consequences of their inaction. This seems to be true for more than just the manager-employee relationship. For example, have you ever worked with a planning committee member who didn't take the committee's work seriously? Then, as a result of this clearly irresponsible behavior, someone else had to "take over" and get things done at the last minute. If you have been involved in such a situation, how did you feel about the committee member who didn't get the job done? Would you depend on that person for a future event? Your relationship with your manager works the same way. Do the things that your manager needs done in timely fashion, regardless of their perceived importance to you, and you will be viewed as a dependable employee.

A mid-level manager once made this observation about one of his peers who he felt would go right to the top. He told me that this person was always trying to answer these three questions:

- What is important to the boss?
- How could he accomplish what was important to his boss?
- How could he make sure his boss knew that he had done the important job?

BE POSITIVE — NO ONE LIKES A COMPLAINER

*Your attitude, not aptitude, will
determine your altitude.*
— Zig Ziglar

When was the last time you actually enjoyed hearing some-one complain? You probably don't enjoy such interaction at all. Managers feel the same way.

So, if you wish to have your boss enjoy dealing with you, use positive words and paint positive pictures. Don't just complain. Instead, offer solutions and suggestions. When you're offering solutions and suggestions, you're not viewed as being negative. People will be more willing to listen to you because they know that you are trying to help them, not tear them or their efforts down. That does not, however, mean that you have to have a suggestion or solution every time you mention something. The object is to be viewed as someone who's willing to help work on problems.

Once during an interview, a newspaper reporter asked me, "Why don't employees appreciate their manager's perspec-tive?" She also wanted to know why some employees are more willing than others to help their manager. "Is it that they just don't get it," she wanted to know, "or is there something else?"

From my observations, it seems that the more positive the employee is as a human being, the more likely it is that he or she will be interested in helping others. It isn't just a matter of "sucking up," since it usually won't matter whether the person they are helping is their manager or a peer. This is no doubt true in other aspects of life as well. One of the best sources on how a positive attitude can make a big difference in your life is Zig Ziglar's *Over The Top*.

A good attitude combined with doing the right things is your ticket to success (assuming, as I mentioned earlier, that you have the "right" product). To illustrate this point, let's look at Figure 4. It shows how your attitude and doing the right things can affect your chances for success.

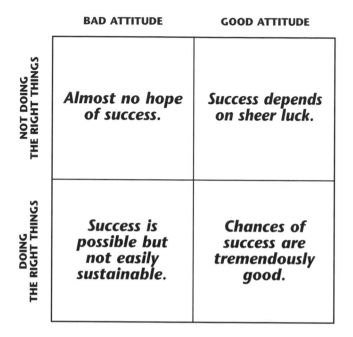

Figure 4: Combining a Good Attitude with Doing the Right Things

Not doing the right things with bad attitude: Virtually no chance of being successful. People in this category tend to be very bitter and cynical. They usually complain relentlessly.

Doing the right things with bad attitude: Sooner or later, the bad attitude will show and limit chances for success. It is highly unlikely that you would be able to "do the right things" on a sustained basis, since doing many of the right things requires a good attitude. Basically, someone with a bad attitude could only "fake it" for a limited time.

Not doing the right things with good attitude: You can compensate for a lot of things with a good attitude. You may even get lucky and be very successful, but at some point you will have to do the right things to remain successful. Typically, people in this category aren't aware of what all the right things to do are.

Doing the right things with good attitude: This is where you want to be. Success is never guaranteed, but when you are doing right things and have a good attitude your chances are tremendously improved.

An interesting aside is that managers have to watch their attitudes, also. A negative or complaining manager can greatly affect the morale of his or her employees. Recently, I was standing in the security check-in line at the Orlando, Florida, airport. Two men behind me were talking about some of the people with whom they worked at some sort of sales organization. One of them mentioned that their boss was a nice guy who had a really good, personable way of working with people.

The other man agreed, but then observed that their boss, while a fine human being, was also a negative, constantly complaining fellow who refused to look on the bright side. He did a poor job of motivating his troops and, in fact, often refused to take an active part in motivating newer employees.

NOTHING IS MORE IMPORTANT THAN GOOD COMMUNICATION SKILLS

If you have poor communication skills, people won't know what you're working on or they won't be able to appreciate what you're doing. Communications skills are what separate the good from the great. These skills also define a major portion of your style, that is, how well you communicate your thoughts and ideas. As you move up the ladder, your communication skills become even more important.

You have to be able to talk to customers and deal with people who work for you. The amount of time and effort you put into communications skills is one of the most important factors, if not the most important, in determining your level of success within your organization. This is impossible to overemphasize. Listen to the feedback you get from your boss and your peers. Go to workshops. Take courses on the subject. Do whatever it takes to become a better communicator. Believe me, it will be the best investment you have ever made.

Remember ... communicating is not just comprised of talking and presenting your own case. Someone in one of my recent seminars asked me to put more emphasis on employees improving their listening skills. He admitted that if he hadn't taken a listening class shortly before attending my seminar, he would not have "heard" my message.

BE WILLING TO TAKE THE INITIATIVE

Don't sit back and wait to be told what to do at every step. Sure, when you first start a new job (or switch to an entirely new area) you may require some "hand holding." After you've been on the job for a little while, however, you should take it upon yourself to investigate problems or issues that affect your job. Managers love people who make managing easier. If your manager has to be involved with every one of your issues (particularly the smaller ones) you will be consuming a lot of that manager's time and making his or her life more complicated. Taking the initiative is how Top Performers really separate themselves from the pack. Often, Top Performers solve problems even before their managers find out that there was a problem. In other words, don't sit around waiting for your manager to direct you. Take that "extra step" to make things happen.

I have heard many managers say that they spend 80 percent of their time with 20 percent of their people. Believe me, you don't want to be among the 20 percent. The people who inhabit that 20 percent usually don't take enough initiative. As a result, their managers view them as more of a liability than an asset.

My own experiences illustrate the preceding point: it was my first assignment after joining AT&T Bell Laboratories. I had been with the company about two months. One day at about five p.m. a friend of mine who had been working there a couple of years dropped by my office. She asked me how things were going. After exchanging the usual pleasantries, I mentioned how I had just found a major problem. I was basically blocked from doing any further testing. I also told her that, since I wasn't completely familiar with the software, I was going to wait until the next day to talk with my project leader about the problem.

At that point, she said rather bluntly, "What do you mean you're going to wait to talk to the project leader? Why aren't you trying to solve the problems yourself? Yes, you're new here, but at your level it is expected that you will get the job done. No excuses."

After I picked my ego up off the floor, I realized that she was right. I should have at least made an effort to investigate the problems to see if I could solve it instead of using the "I'm new here" excuse. I'm sure you know the ending to this story. I stayed late that night, investigated the different areas of the software, and was able to cut and paste together a solution. My project leader was very impressed the next day when I told him about the problem and what I had done to fix it.

LEARN TO WORK WELL WITH OTHERS

Managers love people who are *cool under fire.*

The last thing we want to see is an employee spinning out of control. There is enough excitement in the world; we just don't need any more angst. An agitated and out-of-control employee doesn't do anything positive for the work environment and many times may spread poisonous ill feelings among the staff.

We need people who keep situations under control and are easy to work with. When we describe people who work well with others, we often use terms such as flexible and approachable. Are you willing to listen and compromise or are you thought of as someone who always has to be right? Do you go out of your way to make sure that your team members feel comfortable coming to you for help? It's that "extra step" that determines how effective you will be in the workplace. Also, if you're interested in getting into management, remember that management is rather like a family. How well you work with others will be a big factor in whether you will be invited to join the family.

USE THE "SUCCESS PYRAMID" TO ACHIEVE GREAT CUSTOMER SERVICE

After a recent seminar, a customer service manager told me that he felt my success pyramid would apply directly to building great customer service. After thinking about it as someone who deals directly with suppliers and vendors, I totally agreed with him. Let's look at the pyramid from a customer service perspective (Figure 5). When you are the customer dealing with a company or an individual within that company, wouldn't you want them to be **dependable, reliable, and responsive**? Wouldn't you also want them to focus on **what you think is important**? As you step through the rest of the Success Pyramid, it is easy to see how the pyramid applies equally to managers and customers.

Figure 5: Success Pyramid — What Customers Like to See

WHAT ELSE DOES A MANAGER LIKE TO SEE?

In addition to the six main areas mentioned earlier there are other characteristics that managers like to see in their employees. The list of these valuable characteristics would include the following:

- An understanding of the "three-layer cake with icing" concept.
- An ability to accept and act on negative feedback.
- An eagerness to speak up and share your candid, honest opinions.
- A willingness to be a team player.
- Assertiveness.
- The habit of writing things down.
- A willingness to go "above and beyond the call of duty."

THREE-LAYER CAKE WITH ICING

I hope you will remember these two things: "perceptions are everything" and you have to do the "visible and right things."

I like to use the analogy of a cake. The layers of cake are the real work you do and the icing is the administrative and political things you do. Too many people build five and six layer cakes, with no icing. Think about it. Which cake would you rather have ... a three-layer cake with icing or a five- or six-layer cake with no icing? I take a similar view as a manager. Give me a three-layer cake with icing any day. Believe me, you're much better off building three-layer cakes with icing, because if you're building five-layer cakes with no icing, you're only **working hard** and we already know where "only" working hard gets you.

ACCEPTING AND ACTING ON CRITICISM

Most of us would rather be ruined by praise,
than saved by criticism.
— Dr. Norman Vincent Peale

You have to be able to accept and act on negative feedback. You also have to be able to appreciate how the perception was formed and work on the cause of the perception. Managers like to see that. This is one of the easiest and best ways to impress a manager. When they realize you will act on negative feedback, the whole way they interact with you is going to be different.

If you have problems accepting negative feedback, you should really think about why that is. The problem probably is not that your manager is always wrong. Could it be that your ego is threatened when you get negative feedback? As Michael LeBloeuf put it in his book, *How to Win Customers and Keep Them for Life,* the strongest force in life isn't self-preservation — it's preservation of self-image. Could it be that when you receive negative feedback, it threatens your self-image?

SPEAK UP AND SHARE YOUR OPINIONS

People cannot read your mind.

If you're quiet, they don't know what you're thinking. They will probably assume you have nothing valuable to say. I think many people don't speak up because they feel it's not safe or they're unsure of themselves. As a result, they may feel that they are better off playing it safe than speaking up. I think you're better off expressing your views and opinions. That doesn't mean that you have to be right all the time. People appreciate you for giving your thoughtful comments, speaking up, and just generally being involved. It's part of being a team player. For example, if I'm having a staff meeting with the people who work for me, one of worst things they could do is just sit and stare at me when I ask them a question or ask for an opinion. If no one ever spoke up and shared his opinions, management would be losing a very valuable source of information. We need those views and opinions to help make decisions.

BE A TEAM PLAYER

Help other people.

This concept could involve something no more complicated than simply being courteous to someone else ... or going out of your way to help someone else get his job done.

Do you volunteer to help a colleague if he is having problems getting his job done or do you have to be forced?

Sometimes just taking a few minutes to explain something to someone who is new will create a lasting impression with that person. This goes for your manager as well. Many people mistakenly think that extending a simple courtesy to your manager is "kissing up." For example, your manager is running late for the meeting with your group and he rushes in and explains how he still need copies of the information he wanted to present. What do you do?

A. Look at him as if you can't believe he's late.
B. Pay no attention until he's gotten his act together.
C. Offer to go make the copies for him.

I hope you answered C, since your manager would appreciate any help at that point. No, going to make copies is not like offering to wash his car. It's a simple courtesy that you would appreciate if you were in the same position. It's also part of getting the overall job done. Such actions position you as a selfless team player. If you didn't answer "C" you really should examine why you're not willing to help other people.

One of your team members is about to make a presentation. Then, just before she begins, she says she wishes that she'd had time to get a cup of coffee. What do you do?

A. Laugh and relate to her dilemma.
B. Think to yourself "she needs to quit drinking coffee, anyway."
C. Offer to go get her a cup.

I hope you said C again, because I actually had this happen to me. I have to say that I really appreciated the person who did me that kindness. Getting coffee may not be in your job description, but in a case like this the person who is "under the gun" will appreciate the fact that you did something that you didn't have to do.

The interesting thing about being a team player is that initially it may seem one-sided. That is, you may feel that you are the one who is always "giving," but believe me, over time, team players are remembered by the people they helped. And sooner or later, they will repay the kindness.

BE ASSERTIVE

You have to ask for what you want.

After all, it is your career. If you don't look out for yourself, who will? If you are interested in a new type of job or assignment, tell your manager. In all fairness, you can't expect a manager to know what you want. I can guarantee that the people who "get ahead" ask for what they want. Even if you have told your manager in the past, tell him or her again. Remember that a manager is running around doing a number of different things and working with different employees so expecting a manager to remember exactly what each employee wants can sometimes be a little unrealistic.

Understand that you may not always get exactly what you want from management. There could be perfectly valid reasons why your management refuses your request. Perhaps the short-term needs of the business may require that you not change jobs for awhile. The key here is to inform your manager and work with him or her to make things happen.

Back when I first started working, I found out through frustration that you have to be assertive. I remember going to my manager and telling him I wanted a more challenging assignment. I was frustrated, because I felt that the level of the project I was being asked to do was something I could have done while I was in college. Here I was with a master's degree working on something really quite simple. It just wasn't right, I felt ... a complete waste of talent. I was nervous about going in to see him, because I wasn't sure how he was going to react. I didn't know if I had been given that assignment because of low expectations or because it was the "garbage" assignment you give to the new guy.

I felt that I had to tell him how I felt. I was truly amazed at the response I got. He was completely supportive and positive. It turns out that he wasn't really sure how complex the job was, because at the time he gave me the assignment, the design problem wasn't completely understood. He also confided that since I was just out of school, he didn't want to put me in a overload situation from the beginning. After that I did notice a change in attitude on his part, he went from trying to bring me along easy to an attitude of *"this guy is ready, let's make sure we give him a challenging assignment."*

After our conversation I realized that I never had to worry about how he was going to react when I asked for a more challenging assignment. When you think about it, no manager in his right mind should ever get upset because an employee wants to do more work!

Years ago (before I became a manager), I participated in a panel discussion for high school students. My fellow panelists and I talked about our work experiences and tried to encourage students to consider careers in the sciences. One of the panelists, an African-American engineer from Ratheon, talked about the work he had done and how his career was progressing. He was doing very well indeed. Later, as I was summing up, I mentioned how you have to be assertive and ask for what you want. I pointed out to the students that the only thing the engineer from Ratheon had forgotten to tell them was how assertive he was. I said that even though I didn't know him, I would be willing to bet that he had asked for good, challenging assignments and that most of his career advancements had been generated by some action he initiated. In other words, he didn't sit back and wait for management to tell him or suggest what he should do next. He agreed and thanked me for pointing it out. You see, he wasn't even conscious of how assertive he was himself.

WRITE THINGS DOWN

Here is one of the easiest ways to impress your manager: Simply write down (on paper, e-mail, or whatever) the information you want to provide to him or her. Having written information makes it easier for your manager to digest what you're telling them, plus they will have a handy reference if they need to convey the information to their own manager. By writing things down you convey the message that you are professional and organized.

Look at this way, if you go into your manager's office to provide some status information and it is not written down, what does your manager have to do? Unless she has a photographic memory, she will have to take out paper and pen to take notes and then try to keep up with you while your are rattling off the information. Now, let's say you go in with the information written down, what happens? Your manager listens and may occasionally jot down notes on your write-up. Her level of listening and concentration is much higher and the conversation moves along much faster, because she doesn't have to worry about taking copious notes. You have eliminated the "note taking" worry and freed them to listen.

The wisdom of providing written information is something that we should all learn at an early age. Years ago a local high school sent one of its seniors to "shadow" me during work. I wanted to show him how important it is to write down information you are presenting to management and how impressed management can be when you do that. I showed him the information I was going to be presenting to my department head (my manager's boss). I had a few things scribbled on a notepad, just a little bit of information. I explained that I could just as easily go in and verbally present the information. The boss wouldn't have objected. Instead, though, I got on the computer system and quickly typed the information into a concise "bulleted" list of items. Then I printed up a copy for each of us. We then went into my department head's office and I presented the information. The conversation went very well and my department head even commented on how he appreciated me having the information written.

After we got back to my office the student said, *"You made a believer out of me, it's amazing the difference it made by you having that written down."*

"Writing it down" can be incredibly important to your career, and yet, it's an easy thing to forget about. As a matter of fact, I'd forgotten how important it is myself until I listened to a tape series called *The Secrets of Power Negotiating* by Roger Dawson (see the recommended reading and listening list at the end of this book). He mentions in his program the power of having something written down and how it helps you to get your point across more easily. If you practice the "write it down" technique enough, it will become an almost subconscious habit.

Actually, that's why I recommend studying successful people's styles, as well as asking them outright to divulge their secrets. Many times if you simply ask them for their "secrets of success" they may forget to tell you very important points. Their good habits, you see, have become almost subconscious for them.

A WILLINGNESS TO GO ABOVE AND BEYOND THE CALL OF DUTY

As I mentioned earlier, Top Performers not only do their jobs, they also go out and do additional things. It may be administrative tasks, working on groups, or helping fellow employees get their jobs done. The key here is to understand that when you "do your job," there is a good chance that you are really only doing the minimum requirements. To be viewed as a Top Performer, you have to do more than just your job.

Whatever else you do, do not become someone your managers dread to deal with. Do not have them groaning, *"What now?"* whenever they see you coming. I've asked managers attending my seminars if they'd had employees who made them feel that way. Many said that they had. One candid fellow even admitted, *"I avoid them."*

Being "avoided" in the workplace is not a good way to move your career along.

When you help your manager, not only will your manager appreciate your efforts, but he or she will also remember you when there are opportunities for perks.

When a manager has a perk to pass out, do you think it will end up with somebody he or she dreads to see coming? Of course it won't. The manager is going to give that perk to someone who has been making his or her life easier.

Robert Thomas, who is a retired principal and also happens to be my father-in-law, helped me crystallize this point.

Back when I was first putting together the material for my seminar, I was explaining to him my idea of giving a manager's perspective to employees. I felt that employees were just looking at the problem entirely the wrong way. Since corporate thinking can be very different from the prevalent thinking in a school environment, I wasn't sure if I was even making any sense to him.

After thinking about it for a while, he said that the real difference he saw between the two was that in the corporate setting things happened at a much faster pace. For example, an employee and a manager would probably interact far more frequently than would a principal and teacher. But, for all practical purposes, that is where the differences ended. The interactions between principal and teachers are very similar to those between employee and manager. Many times teachers will have an opportunity, he said, to help the principal get his or her job done. This also happens often in the corporate world. He told me how he'd had teachers who would volunteer during staff meetings to help him with special projects. There were also other teachers who would never help with anything. Usually these were the same ones who would complain bitterly if he asked them to do something new or different from what they had been doing.

He told me that the very people who would never help or always had a problem, were the first people to come to him and ask if they could work some overtime. You see ... overtime was the top perk that a principal in that school system had to give. The overtime usually involved working during evening school programs, being chaperons, etc. "Did they really think I was going to let them work the overtime," he asked me, "when they hadn't helped me at all or had given me a hassle? I'm giving the overtime to the teachers who helped me!"

Don't forget this: **Managers love people who make their jobs and their lives easier.** That's what it is all about.

Since I've been doing my seminars, I have had a large number of managers from very different professions re-emphasize the point that the complainers and the dissatisfied and disagreeable employees were almost always the ones who wanted special treatment or favors.

Let's continue to build our definition for working smart:

WORKING SMART

- Manage Your Image (Perceptions)
- Improve Your Style
- Be Dependable, Reliable, and Responsive
- Do What Your Boss Thinks is Important
- Take The Initiative
- Improve Your Communication Skills
- Be Positive and a Problem Solver
- Do the Administrative and Political Tasks
- Help Your Manager
- Be a Team Player
- Be Assertive (Ask for What You Want)
- Write Things Down

Chapter 12:
Working with Your Manager

Look over the following three questions. Give yourself some time to think about your answers. Your response to these issues should help you get a feel for the kind of relationship you have with your manager:

1. **Do you interact often with your manager?** If you don't interact very often with your manager that could be a warning sign. You don't want to be a stranger to your manager.

2. **Do you wait until your tasks are completed before informing your manager?** You should keep your manager informed while you're working on tasks. That way your manager can enjoy a comfort level about what's happening. Also, your manager shouldn't have to contact you to ensure everything is okay. It's just a good rule to give status prior to things being completed and without having to be prompted by your manager.

3. **Do you have confrontations when you're discussing performance evaluations?** I certainly hope you don't. If you do, you need to acquire the techniques that will help you avoid having them. The problem with confrontations is that your manager may become defensive or withdraw completely from the conversation. Once your manager feels that he can't give you feedback without having a confrontation, you may not receive the valuable feedback you need.

HOW TO WORK WITH YOUR MANAGER

Getting constructive feedback and improving your relationship with your boss is largely a matter of mastering the following four techniques:

- Communicating with your manager.
- Reaching agreement on job priorities and expectations.
- Seeking immediate and continuous feedback on performance.
- Approaching feedback sessions in a non-emotional and non-confrontational manner.

COMMUNICATING WITH YOUR MANAGER

There are basically three things you can do to improve your communications with your boss.

First, you must always keep your manager informed. As I said earlier, managers live on status information. Thus, if you're not telling your manager what's happening, he or she has no way of knowing what's going on with you and no way of passing that information on to his or her boss.

Equally important, you need to communicate your concerns in a timely fashion. Old news is no news. Don't be shy. If you wait too long, the damage may have already been done and you will have missed your chance to remedy the situation.

Provide your manager with status reports. Jack Canfield (co-author of the *Chicken Soup for the Soul* series) agrees that this is a good habit to acquire.

Canfield says that the best way for you to let your management know exactly what you are doing is to provide a regular (weekly, biweekly, whatever is appropriate) status report. In that status report, you would list your accomplishments for the period, any items with which you have concerns or need your manager's help, and your goals for the next period.

What amazes me about status reports is that many employees dread doing them. If the reports weren't required, they simply wouldn't do them. I have often told employees how status reports really benefit them by showing their manager things they may not otherwise know. That is, in the course of a day an employee may have numerous interactions and help various people get their jobs done. But as your manager, I may be sitting in meetings all day and never see how helpful you are. In essence, a status report gives you a chance to receive credit for your exceptional work. Employees just don't realize the power a status report can have in influencing their manager's perception of them.

The other thing about status reports is that many managers view them as a technique to use when you have a "problem." They also don't realize the positive potential of status reports.

Second, when conflicts arise make sure that you tell your side of the story. For example, if you're having cooperation problems with other people on your team, you have to go to your manager and let your side of the story be known. As I said before, there are a lot of discussions taking place behind closed doors. If you're in a conflict with another employee, you can believe the other side of the story is being told. Don't let the other person's story be the only information available.

Third, don't wait until your concerns or issues reach an "explosive" stage. Don't let things simmer and get "under your skin." Don't let an irritation build up and then one day just say, *"I'm sick of it."*

One of my managers once told me, *"Roland, it seems like the only time we talk is when you come into my office and blow up."* He was right, I'd go into his office and immediately start talking about whatever was bothering me. The good thing about that particular manager was that he could actually deal with those explosions. If I'd had a manager who couldn't deal with those explosions, I would have been in trouble. Don't wait until you have reached the meltdown stage. When something first starts to get under your skin, go and talk about it. That's when you can sit down and have a nice non-emotional, rational discussion about it. Resolve the problem right away. It's usually not as bad as you think it is. When you bring up a problem early, your manager has a chance to work on it. After all, a manager can't work on something she doesn't know about.

A manager attending one of my seminars told me that he couldn't understand why employees let things build up to the point where they will quit their jobs before they'll tell the manager about what is bothering them. He said that he'd just had someone quit suddenly. He hadn't even realized that something was wrong. I know what you are thinking: how could he not have known something was wrong? The person probably gave some signals something was wrong. Well, those "signals" aren't as easy to read as you may think. As I've mentioned several times before, your manager cannot read your mind! If you don't take a problem to your manager, then you must assume that he won't do something about it.

Important advice: Take the risk and talk to your manager. I recently realized how difficult it can be for some employees to speak frankly with a manager. When I started doing my seminars and working on this book, I was only concerned with making sure people didn't let things simmer to the explosive stage

I am not naive, I know there is a certain level of risk you take when you tell your manager something you perceive they don't want to hear. This widespread reluctance, however, is much more prevalent than I ever imagined. Why are people so reluctant to talk to their managers? Here are some reasons I have observed:

- Fear that the manager will perceive the employee as "whining."
- Fear they may not have a valid issue.
- Fear that they will be completely shut out of the "information flow" by their peers.
- Fear that their peers will sabotage their careers.
- Fear that their manager will side with the other person, especially if the other person is a "favorite" of the manager.
- Fear from a past experience causing them to distrust all managers.

I know these reasons could be valid in some cases. In general though, I believe the perceived risk is much greater than the "real" risk. Besides, if you don't express your concerns or views, you may be worse off in the long run. Here again, "silence may not be golden." If you are silent, the situation may deteriorate so badly that by the time your management does get involved or your side of the story is heard, your image may have sustained substantial and possibly permanent damage. The saying "an ounce of prevention is worth a pound of cure" really does apply here.

Whenever I am working with someone who is reluctant to talk to his manager, I try to get him to look at the situation from two extreme views: 1. What's the worst thing that could happen? 2. What's the best thing that could happen? By this method, I try to get them to see what the real risks are.

Let's examine the first extreme: Your manager does indeed react negatively and your worst fears come true. Did you do the wrong thing by talking to him? I don't think so, although it may look grim at the time. What really happened? You just learned that your manager isn't supportive. Believe me, if your manager is not supportive, you are much better off finding out sooner rather than later. If your manager reacted negatively, then you were already "in trouble" in your manager's mind. You just didn't know it. Armed with this information, you can move on, knowing that staying would have been keeping you in a negative situation that would have eventually taken its toll. From a mental health standpoint, the earlier you find out that you don't have supportive management, the better off you are.

Now let's look at the second extreme. The best thing happens. Your manager listens and offers ideas and suggestions on how to solve the problem. He confirms or dismisses any perception you may have had about the situation and offers his help. You definitely come out a winner. You don't have to worry anymore because you and your manager are working together to correct the situation.

What usually happens, however, is something between the two extremes. Many times the conversation with your manager isn't as bad as you were expecting. Even if there are rough spots, people still emerge with a great sense of relief. Your manager has heard your side of the story and can now reach a more informed conclusion. Second, your manager can now work on a problem, of which she may not have previously been aware. Conversely, if your manager had issues with you, you can now work on them because you now know what they are. Also, the stage has been set to determine if you have supportive management. That is, you will be able to judge by her actions from this point forward if she is supportive or not. Lastly, you can once again concentrate on your work.

Ultimately, it is your judgment call. Looking at the situation from two opposite extremes will, one hopes, provide a better feel for the real risks you are facing.

REACH AGREEMENT ON JOB PRIORITIES AND EXPECTATIONS

Disagreements or misunderstandings about priorities and expectations can cause a lot of miscommunication between you and your manager.

The key is to actively seek out and understand your manager's expectations and priorities. Always ask for a job's priority. As a manager, it's my obligation to get you to accomplish as many tasks as possible. That's my duty, my job. I want to be able to come into your office, ask you to take care of something, and hear you say, "yes." You may be assured that I'm going to keep coming back until I hear you say, "no." Managers can be merciless that way. What you have to do is ask for priorities. You see, eventually there will be conflicts with your other assignments. If you don't have your priorities firmly set, you will end up disappointing your boss.

So what should you do when your list of assignments, prioritized though they may be, is just too long to complete? You have to stop your manager and ask, *"What's the priority of this new assignment? I have these five things already and this latest one will affect the others. I know you're busy, but it would really help a lot if you would prioritize them."*

Setting priorities is the manager's job. You should avoid making priority calls on your own. The danger is that you may not be doing what your manager thinks is most important. Let your manager make the priority calls and you're safe. Everything will be clear and there will be no confusion between you and your manager.

Also, make sure you completely understand all job expectations. Here's an example: suppose I walk into your office and say, *"I need Job Number Six done."* Job Number Six could be a two-day job, or a two-week job or even a two-month job. How do you know the expectation or quality level that's expected for Job Number Six? Let's say you go off and spend two weeks doing brilliant work on that particular job, which, you come to find out, I had in mind as a four-day. You'll have spent too much time working on that assignment and put in a quality level that wasn't required or needed. Worst of all, missing my deadline (explicit or implicit), won't help bolster my perception of you.

Here again, a lot of trouble could have been avoided if you had simply stopped me and asked, *"What quality level are you expecting on this job? Are we looking at a two-day job or a two-week job ... or what?"* Insist that I explicitly state the expectations. You then restate those expectations to ensure that there's no confusion. After you and I agree, you can do your job with confidence, because you know that you're not only doing what I think is most important, but you're also doing it the way I want it done.

SEEK IMMEDIATE AND CONTINUOUS FEEDBACK ON PERFORMANCE

My attitude is that you have a right to hear constructive feedback more than once or twice a year.

Feedback is not just for annual performance evaluation time. You should be getting the feedback you need all during the year. There shouldn't be the "zap" treatment as described in *The One Minute Manager* by Spencer Johnson and Kenneth Blanchard. (The Zap treatment is when your manager has negative feedback to give you, but never gives you any indication that anything is wrong. Then, at the end of the year at performance evaluation time, he "Zaps" you with the negative stuff.) As Johnson and Blanchard say, you shouldn't have to wait until the end of the year to find out about something you could have corrected early in the year. Ask your manager to give you feedback as you go through the year. I call it "real-time" feedback. That way, you have an opportunity to improve your performance as soon as possible. The beauty of real-time feedback is that by addressing performance issues early, you can often change the potential outcome of your end-of-year performance evaluation.

Don't expect that all of this real-time feedback is going to be praise and pats on your back. You should seek out negative feedback even more enthusiastically than positive feedback. After all, if you don't receive negative feedback, you can't improve. Actually, if your feedback sessions provide only positive comments, but you're not getting the credit you deserve, there's a good chance that you're not being told the "whole truth."

In anyone's performance there must certainly be areas for improvement. You don't necessarily have to be doing anything wrong to have areas for improvement. To grow professionally requires negative feedback. Encourage your manager to tell you how you can improve, how you can make his or her job easier. Your manager will be impressed with your willingness to improve and you will be fixed in his or her mind as a serious worker who is going places.

In Appendix II, I have provided a worksheet you can use to guide performance evaluation discussions between you and your manager. When you look over this worksheet, you will realize that it is very comprehensive. It requires a great deal of self-inspection on your part and will definitely require your manager to really think about how he or she views your performance. I like to say jokingly that there is "nowhere to hide." Virtually every aspect of your job performance is covered. Since I have used this worksheet for many years now, I can tell you that the discussion generated by this worksheet can be challenging, but it is very rewarding. For me, it is simply the best performance evaluation tool I have ever used.

Also, **don't be confrontational when receiving feedback.** The last thing you want to do is make your manager feel uncomfortable during a feedback session, whether it's a formal annual evaluation or a spur-of-the-moment comment. Once that happens, you will stop the "feedback loop," because your manager is now too busy trying to deal with you and your behavior to give you the honest, helpful feedback you need. Remember that your reaction to feedback is the most important factor in determining how much and what type of feedback you will receive from your manager in the future.

HOW TO HANDLE FEEDBACK SESSIONS AND PERFORMANCE DISCUSSIONS

What's the objective of a feedback session? It's to obtain honest feedback. We've talked already about the obstacles: irrational or emotional behavior or an unwillingness to listen. To help you get the most of feedback sessions, there are three areas I'm going to cover:

1. How to approach feedback sessions
2. What to do when you disagree with negative feedback
3. What to do if your manager is displeased with your performance

HOW TO APPROACH FEEDBACK SESSIONS

An angry person opens his mouth and closes his mind.
— Kato

Remember most of all that YOU have to set the stage. You will get very little out of your feedback sessions if you approach them in an angry, emotional, or defensive state.

There is a good chance that your manager will be nervous or even reluctant about giving you (or anyone else) feedback. Maybe she's been beaten up in the process before. It's up to you to ensure that your manager feels comfortable during the session. You may be thinking, *"Why should I be concerned about my manager's comfort level during a feedback session? After all, she's the one in the power position."* I can understand why you may feel this way. The problem, however, is that you're the one who needs the feedback and if you don't get it, you lose! Therefore, the onus is on you to set the stage.

The first thing you should do is let your manager know that you're willing to accept negative, as well as positive, feedback. That will tend to alleviate some fear and discomfort. Second, during the discussion you should listen to all points and comments before you start talking. Do not get defensive or start talking immediately. Let your manager express his or her views and give you the feedback.

Lastly, after your manager is done, start talking in terms of perceptions and opinions. Do not get hung up on the facts. Feedback is a matter of perceptions. If you get hung up on the facts, a couple of things will happen: you and your manager will be forced to defend your positions. Then the ensuing argument will obscure the very useful message that is part of any good feedback session. Don't say things like, *"No, I know I did this job this way"* or *"I know I'm doing a better job than you say I'm doing."* Talk only about "perceptions." That's where you'll find the real message. After all, your manager formed those perceptions and opinions based on something. The real message or feedback has to do with the reasons they formed those perceptions and opinions. Once you know their reasons, you'll know what you need to do to improve. Many times the real message is a great deal different from the original feedback.

WHAT TO DO WHEN YOU DISAGREE WITH NEGATIVE FEEDBACK

The first thing you have to do is keep your cool! Second, you have to keep the conversation centered on words like perception and opinion. Lastly, when you're talking through it, you want to use non-confrontational phrases and questions.

Don't get me wrong, you will always have to do a certain amount of defending. You should definitely tell your side of the story. However, it's the way you tell it that's important. You should say things like, *"I'd like to give you my view of it,"* or *"Could you tell me the events that led to your conclusion?"* The object is to find out what caused your manager to come to that conclusion. Prompt your manager to tell you how the negative perception was formed. Once you've settled that question, ask how you can avoid a similar negative perception in the future. The answer to this question will give you a lot of helpful information and clues as to how the perception was formed in the first place. I have also found it useful to ask the manager, *"How would you have done this job?"*

Usually, this question gets your manager to thinking about what he really felt you did wrong and how he would have handled it. Such questions also imply respect on your part and can help keep the conversation on a friendly, rational, non-emotional level.

WHAT YOU SHOULD DO IF YOUR MANAGER IS DISPLEASED WITH YOUR PERFORMANCE

Again, the first thing is to keep your cool. This type of feedback session is tough, because your manager's point of view is obviously going to differ vastly from yours.

In this situation, use the techniques I discussed above to get as many specifics as possible. Then try to get your manager to separate the facts from the perceptions. Remember, it's the perception you have to understand. Sometimes to keep the discussion on a rational and non-emotional level, you may have to use the "agree to disagree on the facts" technique. You and your manager may have to say, *"Okay, we know we'll never agree on the facts. Let's agree on that, at least, and then let's move on and try to address what we can do about the situation."* It's better to approach the situation this way, because if you try to sit there and argue about the facts, that's exactly what the conversation turns into ... an argument. At that point, the session will undoubtedly go completely downhill.

Sometimes you just have to agree that you're going to disagree on a particular fact.

No one is immune to negative feedback. Once, during a feedback session, my manager told me that he just didn't like the way I'd been handling a certain job. I was really surprised because I thought I had been doing a good job. As we talked, I tried to follow my own advice and avoid getting too hung up on the facts.

To accomplish this, I kept the conversation centered on identifying and understanding the perception, why he felt that way, and how or why he had reached that conclusion. I soon discovered the root of the problem. I hadn't been giving him enough status information. As a result, he didn't really understand how I had been doing the job. In the absence of adequate status information, he based his conclusions about my performance strictly on what he "saw." Unfortunately for me, it didn't look so good. If I hadn't kept the conversation centered on perceptions, I never would have been able to discover the real problem. I asked him, *"How would you have done this?"* and *"How would you like for me to handle it in the future?"* It was the answer to those questions that brought out the real message about status information. I then knew what I needed to do. After that conversation, I made a concerted effort to give him all the status information he needed. After a few months of this deluge, our relationship changed. He had a totally different view of how I was doing my job. I hadn't really changed the basic way I was doing my job. But he now knew what I was doing. It amazed me how simple the root problem was. His lack of information gave him the impression that I was not doing the job. All it took was a change in my style of giving status. A style change. Something else happened at the end of that meeting that really shocked me. My manager told me that he couldn't have had a similar discussion with some of my peers. Why was I shocked? I was already a manager at that time and I couldn't believe that there were managers who didn't know how to take feedback the right way.

In summary, here are the main points of working with your manager:

- Always keep your management informed.
- Seek immediate and continuous feedback. Make it a constant thing, the whole year.
- Don't be someone your manager dreads to see.
- Always try to understand how the perception was formed. Perceptions are at the root of most problems people have.
- Always keep your cool.

NOW, LET'S COMPLETE OUR DEFINITION OF WORKING SMART

- Manage Your Image (Perceptions)
- Improve Your Style
- Be Dependable, Reliable, and Responsive
- Do What Your Manager Thinks is Important
- Take The Initiative
- Improve Your Communication Skills
- Be Someone Who Works Well with Others
- Be Positive and a Problem Solver
- Do the Administrative and Political Tasks
- Help Your Manager
- Be a Team Player
- Be Assertive (Ask for What You Want)
- Write Things Down
- Keep Your Manager Informed
- Seek Immediate and Continuous Feedback
- Stay Cool!

Remember that this new definition of working smart is meant to complement and not replace existing definitions.

Chapter 13:
Closing Comments

> ***Never give up, for that is just the place and
> time when the tide will turn.***
> —Harriett Beecher Stowe

Much of the advice I have given you in this book consists of making simple changes to the way you operate. Nevertheless, those changes will not necessarily be easy to make. Change isn't easy, but it's often well worth the struggle. Many times I have to tell myself to listen to my own advice.

With that in mind, I would like to close this book by reminding you that life is a balancing act. Learn to balance your career and your family. Don't confuse "assertive" with "aggressive." Don't mistake "speaking up" for "talking too much." Giving suggestions freely does not make you pushy or overbearing.

Never lose track of the other person's perspective. It won't always be easy. As I said earlier, the changes themselves are simple, but they may go against years of habits. Don't get discouraged if you occasionally back-slide. Always remember your objective!

Invest in yourself! Don't stop with this book. Study my recommended list and be on the look-out for motivational programs. Never stop learning.

Develop your whole self. I used to wonder if motivational programs had any real value. I think my biggest problem was that I was only interested in developing my technical side. Once I realized that there was a lot more to me than just the technical side, I started to appreciate motivational programs. One day while listening to Brian Tracy, I made the connection that motivational and development programs were just ways of sharing individual discoveries so that we all could benefit. I also realized that to read one good motivational book and say *"I'm done"* is like reading one math book and saying *"I know everything I need to know about math."*

My only regret is that I started so late!

Warning Sign: When you start thinking you know everything, I can guarantee you don't!

RECOMMENDED RESOURCE

You can obtain a good style and personality self-test book-let, "Strength Deployment Inventory," from Personal Strength Publishing, 310-454-5915.

RECOMMENDED READING

- *Over The Top* by Zig Ziglar
- *How to Win Friends and Influence People* by Dale Carnegie
- *Live your Dreams* by Les Brown
- *The Seven Habits of Highly Effective People* by Steven Covey
- *The One Minute Manager* by Spencer Johnson and Kenneth Blanchard
- *How to Gain Power and Influence* by Tony Alessandra
- *Office Politics: Seizing Power and Wielding Clout* by Marilyn Moats Kennedy
- *Skills for Success* by Adele Shields
- *The Seven Spiritual Laws of Success* by Deepak Chopra
- *The Adaddin Factor* by Jack Canfield and Mark Victor Hansen

Appendix I
Style Worksheets

You should make copies of these worksheets for both you and your manager.

Manager:

The purpose of the worksheets is to facilitate dialogue between you and your employee concerning his/her *style,* where style is defined as your perception of this person's work behavior and image. The goal of the exercise is to enable the person to "see" himself/herself as you do. Our research has found that performance discussions tend to miss the very subtle aspects of a person's style and image as it influences his/her job performance.

Your frank and honest impressions are essential to the success of this exercise. Since this person has read the book (or attended the seminar), *Beyond Performance: What you* really *need to know to succeed in the workplace,* he/she wants and is prepared for honest feedback. He/she is sincerely interested in working with you to understand how any perceptions you may have were formed and what he/she can do to improve his/her image and style.

MANAGER DIRECTIONS:

Please check any phrase that best describes your perception of the person in each category. Multiple phrases may apply for some categories. Please feel free to add any descriptions you feel are more representative of your perceptions.

Employee:

Now that you have read the book (or attended the seminar), *Beyond Performance: What you* really *need to know to succeed in the workplace,* you are ready for an interactive dialogue with your manager to obtain feedback on how your style influences your job performance.

After your manager has had time to complete his/her checklist, establish a two-way dialogue to obtain valuable, constructive feedback in a non-threatening way. To explore each point of view:

• Request input, using open questions to learn your manager's perspective. Probe for specific facts that influence that perspective.

• Listen actively to the responses.

• Give your input to explain your perspective.

• Together, explore options on how you can improve any areas needing improvement.

• Agree on what resources are available to you to strengthen areas needing improvement.

• Agree on when to have a follow-up meeting in the future to discuss progress.

EMPLOYEE DIRECTIONS:

1. Have your manager or supervisor fill out a set of worksheets, while you independently fill out a separate set of worksheets.

2. Please check any phrase that best describes you in each category. Multiple phrases may apply for some categories.

3. Add any descriptions you think are more representative of you.

4. Once completed, schedule a meeting with your manager to compare and discuss how each of you answered each category. Remember, for areas where you and your manager disagree, focus on how the perception was formed.

INTERPERSONAL SKILLS

Interactions with Peers

☐ Too quiet — does not speak up and express ideas
☐ Tends to dominate conversations
☐ Overly critical
☐ Supportive — helps others express their ideas
☐ Can be overbearing on occasions
☐ Good listener

Interactions with Immediate Manager

☐ Tends to be quiet
☐ Is confrontational at times
☐ Does excellent job of communicating ideas at appropriate level
☐ Gives too much detail
☐ Have to pry for information — not vocal enough
☐ Too vocal
☐ Good listener

General Management Interactions

☐ Too quiet — doesn't speak up
☐ Communicates at appropriate level
☐ Gives too much detail
☐ Does not give enough detail
☐ Too vocal
☐ Good listener

INTERPERSONAL SKILLS continued

During Meetings

- ☐ Does not listen to others — too opinionated
- ☐ Listens, but needs to improve listening skills
- ☐ Speaks up at appropriate times
- ☐ Communicates ideas effectively
- ☐ Tends to give too much detail
- ☐ Wants to have the last word
- ☐ Talks too much, slows down meetings
- ☐ Reluctant to share ideas
- ☐ Too quiet, rarely speaks up
- ☐ Tries to involve everyone in conversation
- ☐ Appears uninterested in participating in meetings
- ☐ Has tendency to be confrontational
- ☐ Sometimes blows things out of proportion — makes big deal out of small things
- ☐ Tends to be on the attack
- ☐ Good at keeping meeting on track and under control
- ☐ Tends to be too emotional when discussing topics

ATTITUDE

General
- ☐ Very proactive and positive
- ☐ Tends to look at negative side of situations
- ☐ Tends to create or spark negative feelings on team
- ☐ Promotes good teamwork
- ☐ Quick to over react
- ☐ Talks before thinking
- ☐ Has self-interest in mind
- ☐ Willing to volunteer and work issues
- ☐ Not willing to listen
- ☐ Unwilling to compromise
- ☐ Tends to be defensive

Attitude Towards Feedback
- ☐ Doesn't accept negative feedback
- ☐ Readily accepts feedback and acts on it
- ☐ Listens, but doesn't act on feedback
- ☐ Very defensive
- ☐ Tends to be defensive
- ☐ Wants to blame others for situations
- ☐ Unwilling to listen to both sides of story

COMMUNICATION SKILLS

Oral
- ☐ Does not talk — quiet
- ☐ Talks too much
- ☐ Talks too loudly
- ☐ Does not give impression of being knowledgeable when discussing topics
- ☐ Communicates well in informal or one-on-one situations
- ☐ Communicates well in formal situations
- ☐ Tends to be quiet in formal situations
- ☐ Seems overconfident and arrogant
- ☐ Tries to impress with words and terminology
- ☐ Does not communicate well in formal situations

Written (Letters, Memos, Etc.)
- ☐ Delivers work in timely fashion
- ☐ Slow turn-around
- ☐ Tends to be unorganized
- ☐ Often requires a lot of re-work
- ☐ Produces little written work — seems to avoid
- ☐ Have to constantly ask for assigned items
- ☐ Very responsive to requests for written information
- ☐ Does not communicate ideas well in documents
- ☐ Tends to have inappropriate level of detail
- ☐ Well written and organized
- ☐ Communicates clearly and at appropriate level
- ☐ Has problems with grammar

Presentation Skills
- ☐ Appears to be very nervous while making presentations
- ☐ Appears confident and knowledgeable
- ☐ Doesn't seem confident
- ☐ Presentations are not at appropriate level
- ☐ Information is always organized and at appropriate level

IMAGE

Dress
- ☐ Dresses too casually
- ☐ Dresses appropriately
- ☐ Tends to overdress — too formal
- ☐ Sometimes too casual for special occasions or meetings

Body Language/Facial Expressions
- ☐ Too intense
- ☐ Appears uninterested in discussions
- ☐ Limited eye contact during one-on-one discussions
- ☐ Seems to have negative disposition
- ☐ Upbeat and positive
- ☐ Good eye contact during discussions

Miscellaneous
- ☐ Too jovial, doesn't take work seriously
- ☐ Needs to "lighten up" — too serious
- ☐ Just right — appropriate mix of work and play

RESPONSIVENESS

- ☐ Acts quickly on assignments or tasks
- ☐ Delivers all work in a very timely fashion, no matter how small
- ☐ Constantly requires management follow-up
- ☐ Delivers big jobs on time, but tends to be slow with small items
- ☐ Always late
- ☐ Rarely delivers jobs, even small ones, ahead of schedule
- ☐ Usually responds within appropriate time
- ☐ Does not follow-up appropriately on calls and messages
- ☐ Excellent follow-up
- ☐ Sometimes requires management follow-up on tasks

DEPENDABILITY AND RELIABILITY

- ☐ Dependable in every aspect — never have to worry about tasks being done
- ☐ Dependable only in certain situations
- ☐ Have to double-check status of tasks on occasions
- ☐ Always have to double-check status of tasks or assignments
- ☐ Have to check on administrative tasks
- ☐ Have to check on tasks known to be disliked

Appendix II
Performance Evaluation Discussion Guide

You should make copies of this guide for both you and your manager.

Directions:

As with the style worksheets, you and your manager should fill out the guide separately and then get together to discuss your answers. Remember the purpose of this guide is to stimulate discussion on specific areas of your performance. As you might expect, the real value of this guide will be in the areas where you and your manager have different opinions.

Please check the phrase that best describes your performance level in each category. In some cases you may fall between two categories. Please feel free to add any descriptions you feel are more representative of your performance.

Teamwork

- ☐ Inspires good teamwork and through his/her efforts enables significant progress
- ☐ Quick to volunteer assistance and contribute to team effort
- ☐ Generally works well with others and assists in team effort
- ☐ Seldom assists others
- ☐ Unwilling to work with or assist others

Quality Improvement

- ☐ Champions to improve process
- ☐ Works to improve process
- ☐ Identifies problems in process
- ☐ Neutral to process
- ☐ Only complains about process

Quality of Work

- ☐ Outstanding
- ☐ Consistently good
- ☐ Sometimes unsatisfactory

Affirmative Action/Diversity

- ☐ Outstanding contributor and role model
- ☐ Good contributor
- ☐ Supports positively
- ☐ No contribution
- ☐ Negative impact

Dependability

- ☐ Dependable in all aspects
- ☐ Dependable in most respects
- ☐ Occasionally undependable
- ☐ Frequently undependable

Technical Expertise

- ☐ Expert
- ☐ Significant technical growth
- ☐ Has maintained technical competence
- ☐ Not at par with new employees

Initiative

- ☐ Often takes initiative to expand assignment
- ☐ Sometimes enhances assignment
- ☐ Handles job details satisfactorily
- ☐ Requires careful job definition
- ☐ Requires constant guidance and pressure

Resourcefulness

- ☐ Anticipates and successfully meets emergencies
- ☐ Usually finds ways to meet emergencies
- ☐ Occasionally devises ways to handle unusual situations
- ☐ Needs help to handle irregularities

Responsiveness

- ☐ Acts quickly on action items or assignments
- ☐ Usually responds within appropriate time
- ☐ Sometimes requires management follow-up
- ☐ Constantly requires management follow-up

Planning

- ☐ Organizes work of team
- ☐ Effectively plans own work
- ☐ Needs help to plan own work
- ☐ Requires constant guidance

Independence

- ☐ Sets own direction
- ☐ Handles bounded assignments
- ☐ Needs direction

Quantity

- ☐ Frequently exceeds expectations
- ☐ Sometimes exceeds expectations
- ☐ Meets expectations
- ☐ Sometimes below expectations
- ☐ Frequently below expectations

Timely Completion
- ☐ Always meets schedules
- ☐ Usually meets schedules
- ☐ Sometimes meets schedule
- ☐ Seldom meets schedules

Accepts Responsibility
- ☐ Accepts responsibility for issues outside of direct assignment
- ☐ Accepts responsibility for issues related to direct assignment
- ☐ Accepts responsibility when directed
- ☐ Does not accept responsibility

Versatility
- ☐ Does well on several unrelated jobs
- ☐ Can do several related jobs
- ☐ Competent on own job
- ☐ Difficulty with own job

Oral Communication
- ☐ Effective speaker
- ☐ Satisfactory
- ☐ Needs improvement
- ☐ Ineffective

Listening
- ☐ Excellent listener
- ☐ Satisfactory
- ☐ Needs improvement
- ☐ Ineffective

Leadership
- ☐ Encourages expression of alternate ideas
- ☐ Encourages follower independence
- ☐ Only wants people on the team who agree with him/her

Follows
- ☐ Willingly expresses alternate ideas and questions leader
- ☐ Follows only and never questions
- ☐ Undermines team goals

Enthusiasm

- ☐ Improves group morale
- ☐ Enthusiastic
- ☐ Satisfactory/average
- ☐ Lowers group morale

Innovation

- ☐ Provides broad range of ideas to group
- ☐ Produces innovative work
- ☐ Contributes occasional ideas
- ☐ Does not contribute ideas

Written Communication

- ☐ Well written and organized
- ☐ Satisfactory and requires little editing
- ☐ Sometimes unsatisfactory
- ☐ Often unsatisfactory

Effort

- ☐ Consistently a hard worker
- ☐ Sometimes a hard worker
- ☐ Applies minimal effort

Documentation

- ☐ Documents potential work and ideas
- ☐ Documents all jobs
- ☐ Documents most work
- ☐ Avoids documenting
- ☐ Over-documents

Negotiation

- ☐ Always tries to achieve win-win solutions
- ☐ Occasionally tries to achieve win-win solutions
- ☐ Assumes win-lose position

About the Author

Roland D. Nolen has more than 20 years of experience in dealing with the issues and personalities of Corporate America. He has worked as both employee and manager at such well-known companies as IBM, AT&T, and Lucent Technologies. *Beyond Performance* is the direct result of Mr. Nolen's desire to share his hard-earned insights and to help employees achieve a higher level of success. He has conducted seminars for major corporations and national organizations, and has been the guest on numerous talk shows. His *Beyond Performance* Audio Cassette Program is in its 3rd edition.

Mr. Nolen received his B.S. and M.S. degrees from Jackson State University and Purdue University, respectively. He lives with his wife, Terrie, and children, Mallory, Rayna, and Nicolette, in Wheaton, Illinois.

For further information regarding Mr. Nolen's programs on success in the workplace, or to arrange for a live success seminar at your workplace, please call (800) 665-4615. His email address is rnolen@megsinet.net.

Order Additional Copies of *Beyond Performance*

Beyond Performance should be available at your local bookstore, if not, use this order form to mail or fax your order. You can also phone (toll free) to order: **877-2-SUCCEED.**

I want _____ copies of *Beyond Performance*, for a total of: $ _____
1 book: $20   Quantity discounts available

I want _____ copies of the audio program, *Beyond Performance: How Your Professional Image and Working Style Shape Your Success on the Job,* 3rd Edition (three audio cassettes plus two workbooks) at $24.95/each. $ _____

Illinois Residents Tax, 6.75%: $ _____

Shipping & Handling

(Priority Mail) $4.00 + $1.00 for each additional item: $ _____

or (2nd Day) $8.00: $ _____

Total Payment: $ _____

Order (Toll Free): 877-2-SUCCEED

☐ Payment enclosed

    ☐ Bill my: ☐ Visa ☐ MasterCard ☐ Amex

Cardholder Name _____

Card # _____ Exp. Date _____

Signature _____

Name _____

Address _____

City/State/Zip _____

Order Info:

Phone (Toll Free): 877-2-SUCCEED
Fax: (419) 281-6883
Mailing Address: New Perspectives, c/o BookMasters,
PO Box 388, Ashland, OH 44805

"Nothing soothes the working environment quite like the presence of a trusted advisor. Take Roland Nolen's advice and you will be on your way to a better, more relaxed, more productive career."

> Jack Canfield
> Co-author, *Chicken Soup for the Soul* Series

"If you want to earn more money, be promoted constantly and move forward effortlessly ... this great book will teach you all the secrets."

> Mark Victor Hansen
> Co-author, *Chicken Soup for the Soul* Series

"Meeting Planners ask our Speakers Bureau for experts who have been there, done that, and learned from experience. They call that kind of speaker a "Real Person." Roland D. Nolen shares his own business experiences in *Beyond Performance*. They sparkle with truth and wisdom. Buy a box full. You will want to give them to your staff and clients."

> Dottie Walters,
> President, Walters International Speakers Bureau
> Author, *Speak & Grow Rich*

"Most books on how to succeed focus on bosses. This one focuses on the employee and how to manage up. What a great idea to finally show people what it takes to please the boss and get ahead."

> Michael A. Leven
> CEO, US Franchise Systems, Inc.

"What impressed me is Nolen's practical, hands-on approach to career issues. His concepts are very closely aligned to my own personal beliefs and what I have followed in my own career — and it has been very successful for me."

William J. Skeens, Vice-President
Research & Development, Lucent Technologies

"This is a simply stated, easily read book that nonetheless packs a major message. It teaches you how to work on the right things. The information contained in these pages is truly critical to employees getting their fair share, and more, of recognition, economic rewards, and promotions.

Bob Stanojev, Partner
Ernst & Young's Management Consulting Division

"Nolen's philosophy pulls back the covers and offers a good, long look into what management is thinking. This book is critical to your ability to move ahead in your organization. I recommend it highly.

Alisa Speese, Staff Director
McDonald's Corporation

"Nolen's information is very down to earth and can be adapted to a lot of different situations. For a new employee or even a new manager this book is extremely helpful. And, if you're a seasoned person, it may be just the refresher course you've been looking for."

Stephanie Thomas, Assistant Director
Operation/Home Care Program,
Univ. of Illinois at Chicago